Ladies' Home Journal

Easy as 1-2-3

COOKBOOK LIBRARY

Ladies' Home Journal

Easy as 1-2-3

HEARTY MEALS COOKBOOK

by the Editors of Ladies' Home Journal

PUBLISHED BY LADIES' HOME JOURNAL BOOKS

Ladies' Home Journal

Myrna Blyth, Editor-in-Chief
Sue B. Huffman, Food Editor
Jan T. Hazard, Associate Food Editor
Tamara Schneider, Art Director

Produced in association with Media Projects Incorporated

Carter Smith, Executive Editor
Ellen Coffey, Senior Project Editor
Donna Ryan, Project Editor
Bernard Schleifer, Design Consultant
Design by Bruce Glassman

Preface

"Hey, Mom, what's for dinner?" Is that the cry that greets you night after night as you rush in the door after a busy day at work or after completing innumerable household chores? Well, you're not alone. At Ladies' Home Journal we know through the extensive surveys we've conducted that having too much to do and too little time to do it in is the number one problem for women today. We know, as well, that though women like the new options and opportunities they have for varied and interesting lives, they don't want to stint on their domestic responsibilities. When your hungry child asks "What's for dinner?" you want to have an answer—and a real meal on the table that will totally satisfy.

During the last few years at Ladies' Home Journal's test kitchens, we've spent a lot of time trying to solve the problem of lack of time by creating many interesting recipes and time-saving menus that will enable you to get an excellent meal on the table in thirty minutes or less.

We think the quick-to-prepare meals in this Easy as 1-2-3 Hearty Meals Cookbook will delight the whole family. Their stick-to-the-ribs goodness is just what everyone craves at the end of a busy day. For over one hundred years, Ladies' Home Journal has understood and helped solve the problems of American women. I think you'll find the delicious solution to the problems of what to cook tonight in the following pages.

Myrna Blyth
Editor-in-Chief
Ladies' Home Journal

Contents

Introduction

On chilly evenings, light, warm-weather repasts are not enough. It's time for hearty food—like casseroles and spaghetti—the kind of warm-the-cockles-of-your-heart dishes that traditionally simmered on the stove (or baked in the oven) for hours. This tradition need no longer apply—with the help of our Easy as 1-2-3 Hearty Meals Cookbook.

Meat loaf is always an old reliable, but who has time to bake it for the standard hour? You don't—and won't have to with our speedy Micro Meat Loaf, whisked in and out of your microwave oven. What else can you feed the hungry horde? How about Red Beans and Rice with Ham, the New Orleans classic? Or Patty Melt, which takes you right back to your childhood? There's spicy Curry-in-a-Hurry, rich and creamy Three-Cheese Pasta, even a Crab Newburg that won't break the family budget.

We offer some pretty sensational (and speedy) go-along-withs as well: Apple-Spinach Salad, Dilled Peas and Cucumbers, crunchy Parmesan Breadsticks, Confetti Cole Slaw.

And there's even time to whip up dessert—like irresistible Mocha Rum Cake, tangy Lime Dream Pie and Poppy Seed Ice Cream.

No matter whether it's the first chilly evening of fall or a snowy day in February, when the gang demands hearty food, these thirty-six menus will fill the bill.

Sue B. Huffman
Food Editor
Ladies' Home Journal

Green Peppers Stuffed with Hash

A CLASSIC HEARTY MENU

This menu will please the whole family. Spicy hash and corn with herb butter lead up to an ice cream dessert you can put together in minutes. This dinner also serves well on those evenings when people are late getting home and the main dish has to wait in a warm oven.

═══ Menu for 4 ═══

- **Green Peppers Stuffed with Hash**
- **Herbed Corn**

Crusty Rolls
- **Dusty Road Sundaes**

SHOPPING LIST

- ☐ 4   large green peppers
- ☐ 4   ears corn or 1 10-ounce package frozen whole-kernel corn
- ☐ 1   bunch chives or green onions
- ☐ 1   bunch fresh basil or dried basil
- ☐ 1   16-ounce can corned beef or roast beef hash
- ☐ 1   pint fudge ripple ice cream
- ☐ 1   jar caramel topping
- ☐ 1   small jar instant malted milk powder
- ☐ 1   package crusty rolls

Have on Hand

- ☐   Salt
- ☐   Pepper
- ☐   Butter or margarine
- ☐   Chili sauce

SCHEDULE

1. Prepare Green Peppers Stuffed with Hash.
2. Prepare Herbed Corn.
3. Prepare Dusty Road Sundaes.

Green Peppers Stuffed with Hash

4 large green peppers
1 can (16 oz.) corned beef or
   roast beef hash
4 teaspoons chili sauce

Preheat oven to 350°F. Cut tops off peppers and remove seeds; blanch in boiling water to cover 5 minutes. Plunge in cold water to cool. Stuff each pepper with corned beef or roast beef hash and top with 1 teaspoon chili sauce. Bake 20 minutes or until hot.

Herbed Corn

4 ears corn, husked, or 1
   package (10 oz.) frozen
   corn
¼ cup butter or margarine,
   softened
1 tablespoon chopped fresh
   basil or 1 teaspoon dried
1 tablespoon chopped chives
   or green onion
¼ teaspoon salt
⅛ teaspoon pepper

In large saucepot cook corn in water to cover 3 to 5 minutes, until tender. (Cook frozen corn according to package directions.) In small dish combine butter or margarine, basil, chives or green onion, salt and pepper. Serve corn with herb butter.

Dusty Road Sundaes

1 pint fudge ripple ice cream
¼ cup caramel topping
   Instant malted milk powder

Place 1 scoop ice cream in each of four dishes. Top each with about 1 tablespoon caramel topping, and sprinkle with malted milk powder.

STUFFED PEPPER OTHER WAYS

• *In the mood for seafood? Hollow out green peppers; blanch, cool and stuff with diced cooked shrimp, cooked rice, chopped onion, a dash of hot pepper sauce and enough tomato sauce to moisten. Bake 30 minutes at 350°F.*

• *For an unusual treatment of crudites, fill hollowed-out raw peppers with carrot sticks, green onions, celery sticks, radishes and ripe olives.*

• *Use one red pepper half as a dip container for serving with raw vegetables.*

• *Serve cole slaw in raw green pepper cups.*

• *Fill blanched pepper cups with frozen creamed spinach or onions; heat in 350°F. oven 10 minutes.*

• *Hollow out and blanch red peppers; fill with hot whole-kernel corn, chopped broccoli, peas with pearl onions or rice with snow peas.*

Pizza Casserole

CASSEROLE MEAL WITH AN ITALIAN ACCENT

This easy pizza comes to the table in a casserole. No more worrying about the perfect crust! Make your own garlic-bread spread or pick up a prepared loaf at the supermarket and pop it in the oven. Keep the luscious Raspberry Rum Sauce in mind to serve over fresh fruit or ice cream as well as pound cake.

Menu for 4

- **Pizza Casserole**
- **Broccoli Salad**
  Garlic Bread
- **Pound Cake with Raspberry Rum Sauce**

SHOPPING LIST

- ☐ 1 pound ground beef
- ☐ 1 medium yellow onion
- ☐ 1 small red onion
- ☐ ¼ pound fresh mushrooms
- ☐ 1 15½-ounce jar pizza sauce
- ☐ 1 box croutons
- ☐ 1 10-ounce jar seedless raspberry jam
- ☐ ¼ pound mozzarella cheese
- ☐ 1 10-ounce package frozen broccoli spears
- ☐ 1 loaf French bread
- ☐ 1 pound cake

Have on Hand
- ☐ Sugar

- ☐ Garlic
- ☐ Bottled oil and vinegar dressing
- ☐ Lime juice or 2 limes
- ☐ Butter or margarine
- ☐ Dijon mustard
- ☐ Rum

SCHEDULE

1. Prepare Pizza Casserole.
2. Prepare Broccoli Salad.
3. Prepare garlic bread.
4. Prepare Raspberry Rum Sauce.

Pizza Casserole

1   pound ground beef
1   medium yellow onion,
      chopped
¼   pound mushrooms,
      sliced
1   jar (15½ oz.) pizza
      sauce
1   cup croutons
1   cup mozzarella cheese,
      shredded

Preheat oven to 400°F. In 2-quart flame-proof casserole, brown beef; pour off drippings. Add onion and mushrooms to casserole; cook 10 minutes. Stir in pizza sauce. Top with croutons and shredded mozzarella. Bake 10 minutes.

Broccoli Salad

1   package (10 oz.) frozen
      broccoli spears
1   small red onion, sliced
⅓   cup bottled oil and vinegar
      dressing
¼   teaspoon Dijon
      mustard

Cook broccoli according to package directions; plunge into ice water to cool. Drain broccoli spears well; halve crosswise. In large bowl combine broccoli and onion slices. Combine salad dressing and mustard. Pour over vegetables and toss to coat.

Pound Cake with Raspberry Rum Sauce

½   cup seedless raspberry jam
2   tablespoons lime juice
2   tablespoons sugar
2   tablespoons rum
2   tablespoons butter or
      margarine
4   slices pound cake

In small saucepan combine all ingredients except pound cake; heat to boiling, stirring occasionally. Serve sauce warm over pound cake or refrigerate until serving time.

ANOTHER QUICK-COOKING SAUCE FOR POUND CAKE OR ICE CREAM

Rosy Ginger Sauce: In saucepan combine 3 cups sliced rhubarb and ⅔ cup sugar; cover and cook 6 minutes, until tender. Add 1 cup sliced strawberries and 1 tablespoon finely chopped crystallized ginger; cook 2 to 3 minutes, stirring; cool.

Sauteed Liver, Onions and Bacon

TRADITIONAL FAVORITE FOR AN ENERGY BOOST

This American favorite pleases the palate while it provides energy and nutrients, especially iron. The zesty Onion Butter accents the liver and onions, but try it also on other meats and fish.

Menu for 4

- **Sauteed Liver, Onions and Bacon**
- **Onion Butter**
- **Chicory-Orange Salad Toss**

Steamed New Potatoes with Chopped Parsley

Sugar Cookies

SHOPPING LIST

- ☐ 1½ pounds beef liver
- ☐ 2 large onions
- ☐ 1 small head chicory
- ☐ 1 bunch fresh parsley
- ☐ 1½ pounds new potatoes
- ☐ 1 small zucchini
- ☐ 2 small oranges
- ☐ 1 package sugar cookies

Have on Hand

- ☐ Bacon
- ☐ Sugar
- ☐ Salt
- ☐ Pepper
- ☐ Salad oil
- ☐ Red wine vinegar
- ☐ Worcestershire sauce
- ☐ Butter or margarine

SCHEDULE

1. Cook potatoes.
2. Prepare Chicory-Orange Salad Toss.
3. Cook Sauteed Liver, Onions and Bacon.
4. Mix Onion Butter.

Sauteed Liver, Onions and Bacon

1½   pounds beef liver
8   slices bacon
2   tablespoons butter or
        margarine
1   large onion, sliced

Cut liver into serving pieces. In large skillet cook bacon over medium-low heat. Remove and drain on paper towels. Drain off all but 1 tablespoon drippings. Add butter or margarine to skillet; heat just until melted. Add onion and cook until tender, stirring occasionally. Remove from pan and keep warm. Add liver to skillet and cook 6 minutes, turning once. Serve immediately with bacon and onions. Top with Onion Butter.

Onion Butter

½   cup grated onion
½   cup chopped parsley
½   cup butter or margarine,
       softened
2   teaspoons Worcestershire
       sauce
½   teaspoon salt

In small bowl mix all ingredients until well combined. Serve with liver and onions.

Chicory-Orange Salad Toss

1½   tablespoons red wine
         vinegar
⅓   cup salad oil
1   tablespoon sugar
¼   teaspoon salt
⅛   teaspoon pepper
1   small head chicory, torn
         into pieces
1   small zucchini, thinly
         sliced
2   small oranges, peeled and
         sliced

In small jar with tight-fitting lid combine vinegar, oil, sugar, salt and pepper. In large bowl combine chicory, zucchini and orange slices. Toss well with dressing.

QUICK DASH OF WORCESTERSHIRE SAUCE

- *Sprinkle it on tomato halves before broiling.*
- *Mix it with ketchup for a quick barbecue sauce.*
- *Use it to season clam, cheese or avocado dips.*
- *Stir into canned soups—vegetable, pea, beef or chowder.*
- *Blend a little into apple cake or gingerbread batter.*

Braised Ham with Spiced Apricots

HAM AND SWEET POTATOES WITH HERB ROLLS

This delicious apricot-spiced sauce turns ham into a special dinner.

Menu for 6

- **Braised Ham with Spiced Apricots**
- **Fresh Asparagus with Lemon Butter**
- **Herb Biscuits**

Candied Sweet Potatoes

Toasted Pound Cake with Walnut Sauce and Whipped Cream

SHOPPING LIST

- ☐ 2 ham steaks (about 1¼ pounds each)
- ☐ 2 pounds fresh asparagus
- ☐ 1 bunch fresh parsley or dried parsley
- ☐ 2 8¾-ounce cans apricot halves
- ☐ 1 pound cake
- ☐ 1 jar walnut dessert sauce
- ☐ 1 8-ounce package refrigerated buttermilk biscuits
- ☐ 2 12-ounce packages frozen candied sweet potatoes
- ☐ ½ pint heavy or whipping cream

Have on Hand
- ☐ Dark brown sugar
- ☐ Whole cloves
- ☐ Dry mustard
- ☐ Dill seed
- ☐ Onion flakes
- ☐ 1 lemon or lemon juice
- ☐ Chopped pimientos
- ☐ Butter or margarine
- ☐ Salt

SCHEDULE

1. Cook frozen sweet potatoes according to package directions.
2. Whip cream for dessert; refrigerate.
3. Prepare Herb Biscuits.
4. Cook Braised Ham with Spiced Apricots.
5. Prepare Fresh Asparagus with Lemon Butter.

Braised Ham with Spiced Apricots

6   tablespoons firmly packed
       dark brown sugar
16   whole cloves
1   teaspoon dry mustard
1½   cups water
2   ham steaks
       (about 1¾ lbs. each)
2   cans (8¾ oz. each) apri-
       cot halves, drained

In large skillet combine brown sugar, cloves, dry mustard and water; bring to a boil. Add ham steaks and apricots. Simmer 5 minutes. Turn ham; simmer 5 minutes longer. Serve with apricots and sauce.

Fresh Asparagus with Lemon Butter

2   pounds fresh whole
       asparagus, trimmed
½   teaspoon salt
¼   cup butter or
       margarine
2   tablespoons lemon juice
1   tablespoon fresh parsley or
       1 teaspoon dried parsley
2   tablespoons chopped
       pimiento

In large saucepan cook asparagus with salt in water to cover 10 to 12 minutes, until tender; drain well. Meanwhile, in small saucepan melt butter or margarine; add lemon juice, parsley and pimiento. Toss asparagus with lemon butter.

Herb Biscuits

¼   cup butter or margarine,
       melted
1½   teaspoons chopped
       parsley
½   teaspoon dill seed
¼   teaspoon onion flakes
1   package (8 oz.) refriger-
       ated buttermilk biscuits

Preheat oven to 425°F. Combine butter or margarine, parsley, dill seed and onion flakes in a 9-inch pie pan. Blend well. Cut biscuits into quarters and swish each piece in butter mixture. Arrange pieces touching in pie pan. Bake 12 minutes or until golden brown. Let stand a few minutes. Break into serving-size pieces.

START WITH REFRIGERATED BISCUITS . . .

- *For quick dumplings, slit biscuits in half and place around a meat casserole for last 10 minutes of baking time.*
- *For speedy "doughnuts," cut a hole in center of each biscuit. Fry in deep fat until golden. Drain and sprinkle with cinnamon sugar.*

Cranberry Pork Chops
PORK CHOPS WITH A BRIGHT FRUITY GLAZE

Cranberry relish has a holiday look and taste, but there's no rule against serving it all year long. Here it adds tang to a top-of-the-stove pork entree. The tasty dessert starts with prepared angel food cake.

Menu for 6

- **Cranberry Pork Chops**
- **Brussels Sprouts with Pine Nuts**
- **Egg Noodles**
- **Mocha Rum Cake**

SHOPPING LIST

- ☐ 6   loin pork chops
- ☐ 1   14-ounce jar cranberry-orange relish
- ☐ 2   10-ounce containers fresh Brussels sprouts
- ☐ 1   small jar pine nuts (pignoli)
- ☐ 1   16-ounce package medium egg noodles
- ☐ 1   angel food cake
- ☐ ½   pint heavy or whipping cream
- ☐ 1   regular-size package instant chocolate pudding

Have on Hand
- ☐   Salt

- ☐   Pepper
- ☐   Cinnamon
- ☐   Salad oil
- ☐ 1   lemon or lemon juice
- ☐   Milk
- ☐   Butter or margarine
- ☐   Instant coffee
- ☐   Rum

SCHEDULE

1. Prepare Cranberry Pork Chops.
2. Prepare egg noodles.
3. Assemble Mocha Rum Cake.
4. Cook Brussels Sprouts with Pine Nuts.

Cranberry Pork Chops

1	jar (14 oz.) cranberry-or-ange relish
1½	tablespoons lemon juice
³/4	teaspoon cinnamon
½	teaspoon salt
⅛	teaspoon pepper
1½	tablespoons salad oil
6	loin pork chops

In small bowl combine relish, lemon juice, cinnamon, salt and pepper. In large skillet heat salad oil. Brown pork chops on both sides. Drain off fat. Add cranberry mixture. Cover and simmer 20 to 25 minutes or until chops are cooked through.

Brussels Sprouts with Pine Nuts

2	containers (10 oz. each) Brussels sprouts
½	teaspoon salt
¼	cup pine nuts (pignoli)
3	tablespoons butter or margarine
1	tablespoon lemon juice
¼	teaspoon pepper

Preheat oven to 350°. In large saucepan cook Brussels sprouts in water with salt 10 to 15 minutes until just tender; drain well. In small baking pan spread pine nuts in single layer; toast in oven 5 to 7 minutes until golden; set aside.

In small skillet melt butter or margarine over low heat; add Brussels sprouts and lemon juice and stir to heat through and coat well. Transfer to serving dish; season with pepper and top with toasted pine nuts.

Mocha Rum Cake

1	angel food cake
2	tablespoons rum
1	cup milk
½	cup heavy or whipping cream
1	tablespoon instant coffee granules
1	package (regular size) instant chocolate pudding

Slice cake into 3 horizontal layers; sprinkle each layer with rum. In medium bowl combine milk, cream, instant coffee and instant chocolate pudding and beat according to package directions. Spread cake layers with pudding mixture and stack. Chill.

EGG NOODLE TIPS

Add variety to cooked noodles by tossing with:
- *butter and toasted slivered almonds*
- *grated Parmesan cheese*
- *small-curd cottage cheese*
- *leftover broccoli florets*
- *bits of cooked ham, pork or bacon*
- *drained tuna chunks and green onions*
- *blanched green and red pepper chunks*

Three-Cheese Pasta

HEARTY PASTA DISH WITH GOOD CHEESE FLAVOR

Cheddar, chèvre and cream cheese combine to add smooth texture and sharp flavor to this casserole pasta dish. Complement this main dish with simple, traditional accompaniments and a fresh fruit dessert.

Menu for 4

Celery, Radishes and Ripe Olives
- Three-Cheese Pasta
- Romaine Salad

Fresh Pineapple Chunks and Blueberries

SHOPPING LIST

- [ ] 1   8-ounce package broad egg noodles or bow-tie pasta
- [ ] 1   bunch celery
- [ ] 1   bunch radishes
- [ ] 1   head romaine lettuce
- [ ] 1   bunch watercress
- [ ] 1   bunch parsley
- [ ] 1   small red onion
- [ ] 1   pineapple
- [ ] 1   pint blueberries
- [ ] 1   small can ripe olives
- [ ] 1   3-ounce package cream cheese
- [ ] 2   4-ounce packages shredded Cheddar cheese
- [ ] 3   ounces chèvre (goat cheese)

Have on Hand
- [ ]   All-purpose flour
- [ ]   Sugar
- [ ]   Salt
- [ ]   Pepper
- [ ]   Ground red pepper
- [ ]   Olive oil
- [ ]   Wine vinegar
- [ ] 1   lemon or lemon juice
- [ ]   Butter or margarine
- [ ]   Milk

SCHEDULE

1. Prepare fruit for dessert.
2. Prepare Three-Cheese Pasta.
3. Trim celery and radishes; arrange with drained black olives.
4. Prepare Romaine Salad.

Three-Cheese Pasta

8   ounces broad egg noodles
     or bow-tie pasta
2   tablespoons butter or
     margarine
2   tablespoons all-purpose
     flour
1   cup milk
1   tablespoon chopped
     parsley
¼   teaspoon salt
     Dash ground red pepper
1   package (3 oz.) cream
     cheese
1¾   cups (7 oz.) shredded
     Cheddar cheese,
     divided
2-3 tablespoons chèvre (goat
     cheese)

Preheat oven to 375° F. Cook egg noodles according to package directions; drain and set aside.

In large saucepan melt butter or margarine over low heat; add flour and cook 2 minutes, stirring constantly. Gradually add milk and cook, stirring constantly, until sauce thickens, about 5 minutes. Add parsley, salt and red pepper. Remove from heat. Add cream cheese, 1¼ cups Cheddar and chèvre. Stir until cheese melts. Stir in noodles. Pour into greased 2-quart casserole. Sprinkle remaining ½ cup Cheddar on top. Bake 15 minutes, until bubbly.

Romaine Salad

1   head romaine lettuce
1   bunch watercress
1   small red onion, thinly
     sliced and separated into
     rings
3   tablespoons olive oil
1   tablespoon wine vinegar
1   tablespoon lemon juice
½   teaspoon sugar
⅛   teaspoon salt
     Dash pepper

Tear greens into bite-size pieces; combine in salad bowl with onion. In jar with tight-fitting lid combine remaining ingredients. Cover and shake well. Toss with salad.

STORING CHEESE

• *Rewrap cheese in its own package; place in an airtight container in refrigerator.*

• *Don't throw away moldy cheese; just scrape off the mold and serve as usual.*

• *Grate edges and loose ends if they dry out; store in a jar for future use.*

Ham and Cheese Pitas

OLD FAVORITES IN A NEW STYLE

On those days when you're too busy to fuss, you can serve this tasty hearty meal, complete with a quick soup. Easy as it is, this menu contains all the elements of a balanced meal—and the kids will love it.

=== Menu for 4 ===

- **Savory Mushroom Potato Soup**
- **Ham and Cheese Pitas**
- **Carrot Slaw**
- **Chocolate Layer Cake**

SHOPPING LIST

- ☐ ½   pound ham
- ☐ 1   small head iceberg lettuce
- ☐ 1   pound carrots
- ☐ 1   large onion
- ☐ 1   8¼-ounce can pineapple chunks
- ☐ 1   4½-ounce jar sliced mushrooms
- ☐ 1   small can or package flaked coconut
- ☐ 1   small package roasted, hulled sunflower seed
- ☐ 4   pita breads
- ☐ 1   chocolate layer cake
- ☐ ½   pound Swiss cheese

- ☐   Sage
- ☐   Thyme
- ☐   Sweet pickle relish
- ☐ 1   lemon or lemon juice
- ☐   Milk
- ☐   Mayonnaise
- ☐   Butter or margarine
- ☐   Raisins
- ☐   Instant mashed potato flakes

Have on Hand

- ☐   Salt
- ☐   Pepper

SCHEDULE

1. Prepare Carrot Slaw; cover and refrigerate.
2. Prepare Savory Mushroom Potato Soup.
3. Prepare Ham and Cheese Pitas.

Savory Mushroom Potato Soup

¼	cup finely chopped onion
2	tablespoons butter or margarine
2½	cups milk
1	jar (4½ oz.) sliced mushrooms, undrained
½	teaspoon salt
⅛	teaspoon pepper
⅛	teaspoon sage
⅛	teaspoon thyme
½	cup instant mashed potato flakes

In heavy saucepan saute onion in butter or margarine until tender. Add milk, mushrooms, salt, pepper, sage and thyme. Bring to a boil. Whisk in instant mashed potato flakes and stir well, adding more if necessary to thicken.

Ham and Cheese Pitas

½	pound ham, diced
½	pound Swiss cheese, diced
¼	cup mayonnaise
¼	cup sweet pickle relish
4	pita breads
1	cup iceberg lettuce, shredded

In medium bowl combine ham, cheese, mayonnaise and relish. Spoon into pitas and top with shredded lettuce.

Carrot Slaw

1	pound grated carrots
⅔	cup seedless raisins
1	can (8¼ oz.) pineapple chunks, drained
⅓	cup flaked coconut
⅓	cup roasted hulled sunflower seed
3	tablespoons mayonnaise
1½	teaspoons lemon juice

In large bowl combine all ingredients. Cover and chill until serving time.

CARROT SLAW VARIATIONS

- *Combine 1 pound shredded carrots, 1 sliced green onion, ½ cup diced red pepper and ¼ cup bottled buttermilk dressing; serve on lettuce leaves.*
- *Combine 4 cups shredded carrots with ½ cup mayonnaise, ½ cup plain yogurt, 1½ teaspoons curry powder, ¼ teaspoon salt, ½ cup raisins and 2 tablespoons chopped mango chutney.*

Salami Frittata

DELICIOUS SALAMI AND EGGS

You can whip up this quick Italian meal in minutes. Keep this salad in mind for your next dinner party; it's especially good with chicken or fish.

Menu for 4

- **Salami Frittata**
- **Bibb Lettuce and Radish Salad**
- **Pizza Bread**

Fresh Strawberries with Confectioners' Sugar

SHOPPING LIST

- ☐ ¼   pound unsliced salami
- ☐ 1   medium zucchini
- ☐ 1   large head or 2 small heads Bibb lettuce
- ☐ 1   bunch radishes
- ☐ 2   medium onions
- ☐ 1   bunch green onions
- ☐ 1   pint strawberries
- ☐ 1   small jar green olives
- ☐ 1   loaf French bread
- ☐ 1   dozen eggs
- ☐ ½   pound sliced Muenster cheese

Have on Hand.

- ☐   Confectioners' sugar
- ☐   Salt
- ☐   Pepper

- ☐   Garlic
- ☐   Salad oil
- ☐   Olive oil
- ☐   Tarragon vinegar
- ☐   Grated Parmesan cheese
- ☐   Dijon mustard
- ☐   Anchovy paste (optional)

SCHEDULE

1. Clean and hull strawberries. Chill.
2. Assemble and bake Pizza Bread.
3. Prepare Salami Frittata.
4. Prepare Bibb Lettuce and Radish Salad.

Salami Frittata

1 tablespoon salad oil
1 medium zucchini, sliced
1 cup chopped salami
1 small garlic clove, crushed
8 eggs
½ cup water
¼ cup grated Parmesan
   cheese

Preheat oven to 350°F. In large ovenproof skillet heat oil over medium heat. Add zucchini, salami and garlic; saute. In medium bowl beat eggs with water and grated Parmesan. When zucchini is tender but not limp, pour egg mixture into same skillet and cook over medium heat 1 to 2 minutes. Place skillet in oven and bake until set, 8 to 10 minutes.

Bibb Lettuce and Radish Salad

1 tablespoon tarragon
   vinegar
1 teaspoon Dijon mustard
½ teaspoon anchovy paste
   (optional)
1 garlic clove, crushed
3 tablespoons salad oil
4 cups Bibb lettuce, washed
   and torn into pieces
1 cup sliced radishes
¼ cup sliced green onions
¼ cup sliced pimiento-stuffed
   olives

In jar with tight-fitting lid combine vinegar, mustard, anchovy paste, garlic and oil; shake well. Combine vegetables in salad bowl. Just before serving, toss with dressing to coat.

Pizza Bread

2 tablespoons olive oil
2 medium onions, thinly
   sliced
½ teaspoon salt
   Dash pepper
1 loaf French bread, halved
   lengthwise
8 ounces Muenster cheese,
   sliced

Preheat oven to 350°F. In small skillet heat oil over medium heat. Add onions, salt and pepper; saute until translucent but not browned. Spread onions on cut surfaces of bread. Lay cheese slices on top and bake on cookie sheet 15 minutes. Cut into pieces.

FAST ZEST WITH GREEN OLIVES

- *Slice and toss into a green salad or a batch of long-grain rice.*
- *Chop and sprinkle over broiled fish before serving.*
- *Slice or chop and add to egg salad.*
- *Chop and stir into gazpacho or lentil soup.*
- *Chop and fold into meat loaf, scrambled eggs or quiches.*
- *Chop finely and mix with sour cream and parsley as dip.*

Patty Melt

FUN SUPPER FOR THE WHOLE FAMILY

These cheeseburgers—rich with tasty Swiss cheese, onions and chili sauce—are sure to be a hit. Make the meal special by turning your counter or sideboard into a salad bar; vary the greens and accompaniments to suit your family's taste. For adults, drizzle orange-flavored liqueur over the quick and delicious dessert.

Menu for 4

- **Patty Melt**
- **Make-Your-Own Salad**
- **Mandarin Pound Cake**

SHOPPING LIST

- ☐ 1 head romaine lettuce
- ☐ 1 head chicory or escarole
- ☐ 1 pint cherry tomatoes or 2 large tomatoes
- ☐ 2 large sweet onions
- ☐ 1 11-ounce can mandarin orange sections
- ☐ 1 20-ounce can chick-peas (garbanzo beans)
- ☐ 1 small package croutons
- ☐ 1 small can or package shredded coconut
- ☐ 1 loaf rye bread
- ☐ 1 pound cake
- ☐ ½ pound sliced Swiss cheese
- ☐ 1 pound ground beef

Have on Hand

- ☐ Salt
- ☐ Pepper
- ☐ Butter or margarine
- ☐ Chili sauce
- ☐ Bottled oil and vinegar dressing
- ☐ Prepared blue cheese dressing

SCHEDULE

1. Prepare Make-Your-Own Salad.
2. Cook Patty Melt.
3. Prepare Mandarin Pound Cake.

Patty Melt

1 **pound ground beef**
   Dash pepper
½ **teaspoon salt**
8 **slices rye bread**
4 **tablespoons butter or**
    margarine
8 **slices Swiss cheese**
½ **cup finely chopped onion**
¼ **cup chili sauce**

Shape ground beef into 4 ovals and flatten to about ½-inch thickness. Sprinkle with pepper. Heat a large heavy skillet and sprinkle with salt. Add patties; brown 2 to 3 minutes on each side for medium rare.

    Spread one side of each bread slice with ½ tablespoon butter or margarine. Top unbuttered sides of 4 bread slices with half the cheese. Top each with 2 tablespoons onion and 1 tablespoon chili sauce. Transfer cooked patties to onion-topped bread. Cover with remaining cheese and bread, buttered side up. Place on hot ungreased griddle or skillet. Grill until golden on both sides, pressing with pancake turner on each side.

Make-Your-Own Salad

1 **head romaine lettuce**
½ **head chicory or escarole**
1 **can (20 oz.) chick-peas**
    (garbanzo beans), drained
1 **cup packaged croutons**
1 **pint cherry tomatoes or**
    2 large tomatoes, sliced

1 **large sweet onion, sliced**
    and separated into rings
   Bottled oil and vinegar
    dressing
   Prepared blue cheese
    dressing

Wash and tear lettuce; place in separate bowls. Place chick-peas, croutons, tomatoes and onion rings in individual serving dishes. Set out all salad ingredients on counter or sideboard and let people assemble their own salads.

Mandarin Pound Cake

4 **slices pound cake**
1 **can (11 oz.) mandarin**
    orange sections
4 **tablespoons shredded**
    coconut

In each of 4 dessert bowls place 1 slice pound cake. Top each with one-quarter of the orange sections and sprinkle with 1 tablespoon shredded coconut.

SALAD BAR FOR A CROWD

Add some or all of these extras to the Make-Your-Own Salad ingredients:
• *crumbled bacon*
• *pickled beets*
• *cucumber slices*
• *crumbled feta or blue cheese*
• *sliced fresh mushrooms*
• *shredded red cabbage*
• *sliced hard-cooked eggs*

Chicken Oreganata

HERBED CHICKEN WITH AN UNUSUAL SALAD

This fragrant and tasty chicken entree will simmer to tender perfection while you prepare the rest of the meal. The salad is high in fiber, iron and vitamins. For color and flavor, toss chopped parsley with the orzo just before serving.

Menu for 4

- **Chicken Oreganata Orzo with Parsley**
- **Apple-Spinach Salad**
- **Creamy Orange Sundaes**

SHOPPING LIST

- ☐ 1 3-pound broiler-fryer, cut into 8 pieces
- ☐ 1 pound fresh spinach
- ☐ 1 medium tart apple
- ☐ 1 small red onion
- ☐ 1 bunch parsley
- ☐ 1 16-ounce package orzo
- ☐ 1 pint vanilla ice cream
- ☐ 1 pint orange sherbet

- ☐   Olive oil
- ☐   Salad oil
- ☐   Cider vinegar
- ☐ 1 lemon or lemon juice
- ☐   Orange juice
- ☐   Raisins

Have on Hand

- ☐   Sugar
- ☐   Cornstarch
- ☐   Salt
- ☐   Pepper
- ☐   Garlic
- ☐   Oregano

SCHEDULE

1. Prepare Chicken Oreganata.
2. Prepare orzo with chopped parsley.
3. Prepare Apple-Spinach Salad.
4. Prepare topping for Creamy Orange Sundaes.

Chicken Oreganata

1   broiler-fryer chicken (3
      lb.), cut into 8 pieces
½   teaspoon salt
⅛   teaspoon pepper
2   tablespoons olive oil
2   garlic cloves, pressed
⅓   cup lemon juice
1   teaspoon oregano
2   tablespoons chopped
      parsley

Sprinkle chicken with salt and pepper. In Dutch oven heat oil. Add chicken and brown on both sides. Remove from heat. Transfer chicken to platter; set aside. To drippings add garlic; saute 1 minute. Add lemon juice and oregano. Return chicken to Dutch oven. Cover and simmer until juices run clear when chicken is pricked with a fork, about 20 minutes. Arrange chicken on serving platter. Spoon on pan juices and sprinkle with parsley.

Apple-Spinach Salad

4   cups fresh spinach leaves
2   tablespoons salad oil
2   tablespoons cider vinegar
¼   teaspoon salt
      Pinch sugar
1   medium tart apple, diced
¼   cup chopped red onion
¼   cup raisins or currants

Tear spinach into bite-size pieces; set aside in salad bowl. In small bowl mix oil, vinegar, salt and sugar. Add apple, onion and raisins or currants; toss to coat. Cover and let stand 10 minutes or longer. Stir apple mixture into salad bowl and toss with spinach until well coated.

Creamy Orange Sundaes

¼   cup sugar
1½ teaspoons cornstarch
1   cup orange juice
1   pint vanilla ice cream
1   pint orange sherbet

In 2-quart saucepan combine sugar and cornstarch. Gradually stir in orange juice. Stirring constantly, bring to a boil over medium heat and boil 1 minute. Remove from heat. Set aside to cool until serving time.

In each of 4 dessert bowls place 1 scoop vanilla ice cream and 1 scoop orange sherbet. Top with ¼ cup orange sauce.

BUYING APPLES

- *One pound of apples will yield about 3 cups diced or sliced.*
- *Available almost year round, apples are at their peak from fall to spring.*
- *Among the best apple varieties for all uses, including salads, are Delicious, Golden Delicious, MacIntosh, Granny Smith, Cortland, Winesap and Jonathan.*

Pitaburgers with Middle Eastern Salad

NEW ACCENT FOR AN OLD FAVORITE

Look in the specialty section of your supermarket for tahini (sesame paste) or find it in a gourmet shop or Middle Eastern food store. The unusual flavor it lends to vegetables will make it worth the search. Served in heated pita breads, these burgers are sure to become a standard.

Menu for 4

- **Pitaburgers**
- **Middle Eastern Salad**
- **Carrots with Cumin**
- **Fruit 'n' Honey**

SHOPPING LIST

- ☐ 1½ pounds carrots
- ☐ 1 large or 2 medium tomatoes
- ☐ 1 small cucumber
- ☐ 1 bunch green onions
- ☐ 1 small onion
- ☐ 1 bunch fresh parsley
- ☐ 1 small bunch grapes
- ☐ 2 medium bananas
- ☐ 4 pita breads
- ☐ 1 20-ounce can pineapple chunks in own juice
- ☐ 1 small jar tahini (sesame paste)
- ☐ 1 8-ounce container vanilla yogurt
- ☐ 1 pound ground beef

Have on Hand

- ☐ Sugar
- ☐ Salt
- ☐ Pepper
- ☐ Garlic
- ☐ Salad oil
- ☐ Cumin
- ☐ Honey
- ☐ 1 lemon or lemon juice
- ☐ Butter or margarine

SCHEDULE

1. Prepare Carrots with Cumin.
2. Prepare Pitaburgers and Middle Eastern Salad.
3. Prepare Fruit 'n' Honey.

Pitaburgers

> 1 **pound ground beef**
> ½ **teaspoon salt**
> ⅛ **teaspoon pepper**
> 4 **pita breads, warmed**

Preheat broiler. Shape ground beef into 4 round patties and season lightly with salt and pepper. Broil to desired doneness, about 5 minutes on each side for medium.

Cut open one end of each pita round. Fill with 1 cooked beef patty and ½ cup Middle Eastern Salad.

Middle Eastern Salad

> ¼ **cup tahini (sesame paste)**
> 2 **tablespoons lemon**
>   **juice**
> 1 **garlic clove, crushed**
> ½ **teaspoon salt**
> 1 **cup chopped fresh**
>   **tomatoes**
> ½ **cup peeled, seeded and**
>   **diced cucumber**
> ¼ **cup chopped green**
>   **onions**
> ¼ **cup chopped**
>   **parsley**

In medium bowl combine tahini, lemon juice, garlic and salt. Stir until smooth. Add tomatoes, cucumber, green onions and parsley; toss.

Carrots with Cumin

> 1 **tablespoon butter or**
>   **margarine**
> 1½ **teaspoons salad oil**
> 1½ **pounds carrots, sliced**
>   **diagonally**
> ⅓ **cup diced onion**
> ¾ **teaspoon ground cumin**
> ½ **teaspoon salt**
> ¼ **teaspoon sugar**
> ¼ **cup water**
> 1½ **tablespoons chopped parsley**

In 10-inch skillet melt butter or margarine with oil over medium heat. Add carrots, onion, cumin, salt and sugar. Saute 1 minute. Add water and bring to a boil. Reduce heat, cover and simmer 10 to 12 minutes, until tender. Top with parsley.

Fruit 'n' Honey

> 1 **cup fresh grapes**
> 2 **medium bananas, sliced**
> 1 **can (20 oz.) pineapple**
>   **chunks in own juice**
> 1 **tablespoon honey**
> 1 **container (8 oz.) vanilla yogurt**

In large bowl combine grapes and bananas. Drain pineapple, reserving ⅓ cup juice. Add pineapple to grapes and bananas. In small bowl stir together reserved juice and honey. Pour over fruit and toss until well combined. Top with dollops of vanilla yogurt.

Hearty Meals Tips

Easy and Pleasing Spaghetti Main Dish

Cook 1 pound spaghetti according to package directions. Meanwhile, in small saucepan heat ½ cup olive oil. Add 2 crushed garlic cloves and cook over low heat until golden, about 2 to 3 minutes. Toss hot cooked spaghetti with garlic oil and ½ cup (1 bunch) finely chopped parsley. If desired, serve with grated Parmesan cheese and/or crushed red pepper.

Know Your Potatoes

There are dozens of varieties of potatoes, but only four basic types. All are good—and good for you. Many of the potato's nutrients are just beneath the skin, so whenever possible, serve them "in their jackets." Scrubbing potatoes with a good vegetable brush under cool running water will clean them quickly and easily.

- *Russet, or baking potatoes, are frequently referred to as "Idaho" potatoes. They do come from Idaho, but also from Washington, Oregon, Minnesota, Maine and New York. Russets are oval-shaped, and their skins are rough-textured. They're fine all-purpose potatoes and superior for baking.*
- *Round reds are smaller than russets and have rosy skins. They're good for boiling and, when "new," are often served whole, skins on.*
- *Round whites are the most common type grown in this country. Size varies according to variety. They're good all-purpose boiling, baking and frying potatoes.*
- *Long whites are all-purpose, too; because of their elliptical shape, they're especially convenient for french frying. Restaurants often select this variety for baking.*

Hearty One-Dish Meal for Kids

Preheat oven to 350° F. Place 3 slices of bologna in each of 3 6-ounce custard cups. Combine a 12-ounce package frozen macaroni and cheese with 1 cup cooked green peas; spoon evenly into each bologna-lined cup. Cover with foil. Heat in oven for about 15 to 20 minutes or until macaroni is heated through. Remove foil during last 5 minutes. Makes 3 servings.

Almost-Instant Chili

In medium skillet or saucepan combine ½ cup ground beef, 1 small chopped onion, a minced garlic clove, 2 teaspoons chili powder, 1½ teaspoons cumin and a dash of crushed pepper; cook over medium heat until meat is browned. Blend in a 16-ounce can or jar of pork 'n' beans and 1 cup tomato juice. Simmer 20 to 25 minutes. Makes 4 servings.

Easy "Eggs Over Easy"

Don't worry about breaking the yolks if your family asks for fried eggs. Just add 2 tablespoons of water to the skillet with the eggs, cover and cook. The eggs will look as though they've been flipped.

Ice Cream Tips

- *By government regulation, ice cream must contain a minimum of 10 percent butterfat and weigh 4.5 pounds per gallon. Most brands contain between 10 and 15 percent butterfat.*
- *Ice cream is lower in calories than many other desserts. Ice cream with a 10 percent butterfat content has 128 calories per ½ cup; with a 16 percent butterfat content ice cream has 164 calories per ½ cup.*
- *To scoop, dip spoon or scoop in cold water first to prevent ice cream from sticking. Shake excess water from scoop to prevent adding ice crystals to the ice cream.*
- *Americans consume nearly 800 million gallons of ice cream and related products annually.*

Spinach Fettucine with Gorgonzola Sauce, page 36

Fettuccine with Gorgonzola

ITALIAN MEAL WITH COLOR AND FLAIR

Bright with color and rich with taste, this dinner seems just too special to be a quickie—but it is.

Menu for 4

- **Spinach Fettuccine with Gorgonzola Sauce**
- **Parmesan Breadsticks**
- **Romaine Salad with Tomatoes, Onions and Cucumbers**
- **Berry-Melon Wedges**

SHOPPING LIST

- ☐ 1 pound fresh spinach fettuccine
- ☐ 1 head romaine lettuce
- ☐ 2 tomatoes
- ☐ 1 medium cucumber
- ☐ 1 medium onion
- ☐ 1 pint strawberries or 1 10-ounce package frozen strawberries
- ☐ 1 cantaloupe
- ☐ 1 8-ounce package refrigerated crescent rolls
- ☐ ¼ pound Gorgonzola cheese
- ☐ ½ pint heavy or whipping cream

Have on Hand
- ☐ Sugar

- ☐ Pepper
- ☐ Bottled salad dressing
- ☐ 1 lemon or lemon juice
- ☐ Parmesan cheese
- ☐ Eggs
- ☐ Cream sherry

SCHEDULE

1. Prepare sauce for Berry-Melon Wedges.
2. Prepare Parmesan Breadsticks.
3. Prepare vegetables for salad.
4. Prepare Spinach Fettuccine with Gorgonzola Sauce.

Spinach Fettuccine with Gorgonzola Sauce

1 **pound fresh spinach fettuccine**
1 **cup heavy or whipping cream**
1 **egg yolk**
¼ **pound crumbled Gorgonzola cheese**
¼ **cup grated Parmesan cheese**
⅛ **teaspoon freshly ground pepper**

In large saucepot cook fettuccine according to package directions. Meanwhile, in medium saucepan heat cream with egg yolk, stirring occasionally, until bubbles form around edge of pan. Add both cheeses; stir until melted. Pour over hot noodles and season with pepper; toss and serve immediately.

Parmesan Breadsticks

1 **package (8 oz.) refrigerated crescent rolls**
¼ **cup grated Parmesan cheese**

Preheat oven to 375° F. Unroll crescent roll dough and divide into quarters, patting seams together to form 4 rectangles. Cut lengthwise into ½-inch strips. Roll in grated Parmesan cheese. Twist strips. Bake on ungreased cookie sheet according to package directions.

Berry-Melon Wedges

1 **cup sliced strawberries**
¼ **cup cream sherry**
3 **tablespoons sugar**
1 **tablespoon lemon juice**
1 **cantaloupe, peeled and cut into 1-inch wedges**

In food processor or blender combine strawberries, sherry, sugar and lemon juice. Process until smooth; refrigerate until serving time. Serve over cantaloupe wedges.

SPINACH PASTA CARBONARA

Enjoy the taste and nutrients of spinach noodles with this quick pasta dish: Beat together 4 tablespoons butter, 4 tablespoons heavy cream and 2 eggs; cook over medium heat until bubbles form. Pour over cooked, drained spinach noodles; top with crumbled cooked bacon and grated Parmesan or Romano cheese.

Roast Beef Sandwich Platter, page 40

Herbed Lamb Chop, page 42   *Stir-Fried Beef and Zucchini, page 44* ▶

Open-Face Roast Beef Sandwiches

ELEGANT AND EASY ENTERTAINING

This tasty sandwich features deli roast beef topped with bacon and seasoned with herbed mayonnaise. Pop fresh berries on mini cheesecakes, with or without a dollop of jam, for a quick and delicious dessert.

Menu for 4

- **Open-Face Roast Beef Sandwiches**
- **Potato Salad with Chives and Pimiento**
- **Asparagus Vinaigrette with Red Pepper**
- **Mini Cheesecakes with Fresh Berries**

SHOPPING LIST

- ☐ 8 ounces sliced rare roast beef
- ☐ ½ pound bacon
- ☐ 1½ pounds fresh asparagus
- ☐ 1 red pepper
- ☐ 1 bunch fresh chives
- ☐ 1 bunch fresh parsley
- ☐ 2 medium onions
- ☐ ½ pint raspberries or strawberries
- ☐ 1 loaf pumpernickel bread
- ☐ 1 small jar gherkins
- ☐ 4 mini cheesecakes
- ☐ 1½ pounds potato salad

Have on Hand
- ☐ Salt
- ☐ Pepper

- ☐ Chervil
- ☐ Tarragon
- ☐ Celery seed
- ☐ Salad oil
- ☐ Red wine vinegar
- ☐ Chopped pimientos
- ☐ Butter
- ☐ Mayonnaise

SCHEDULE

1. Prepare Potato Salad with Chives and Pimiento.
2. Prepare Asparagus Vinaigrette with Red Pepper.
3. Prepare Open-Face Roast Beef Sandwiches.

Open-Face Roast Beef Sandwiches

6	*tablespoons mayonnaise*
¾	*teaspoon chervil*
¾	*teaspoon tarragon*
¾	*teaspoon chopped chives*
¾	*teaspoon chopped fresh parsley*
4	*slices bacon*
1	*medium onion, thinly sliced*
1½	*tablespoons butter, softened*
4	*slices pumpernickel bread*
8	*ounces sliced rare roast beef*
4	*gherkins*

In small bowl combine mayonnaise with herbs; set aside. In medium skillet cook bacon until crisp; drain and set aside. To hot drippings in skillet add onion and saute, stirring frequently, until golden brown; drain. Spread each slice of bread with 1 teaspoon each butter and herbed mayonnaise. Add roast beef. Top with bacon, onion, gherkin and another dab of herbed mayonnaise.

Potato Salad with Chives and Pimiento

1½	*pounds potato salad*
3	*tablespoons chopped chives*
3	*tablespoons chopped pimiento*
½	*teaspoon celery seed*

In large bowl combine potato salad, chives and pimiento. Sprinkle celery seed over salad.

Asparagus Vinaigrette with Red Peppers

1½	*pounds asparagus, trimmed*
2	*tablespoons salad oil*
1½	*tablespoons red wine vinegar*
2	*teaspoons finely minced onion*
½	*teaspoon salt*
⅛	*teaspoon pepper*
2	*tablespoons finely diced red pepper*

In large skillet cook asparagus in boiling salted water until tender. Plunge into ice water to cool. Remove and drain on paper towels. In small bowl combine oil, vinegar, onion, salt and pepper. Arrange asparagus on serving platter; top with red pepper. Just before serving pour dressing over vegetables.

OPEN-FACE SANDWICHES

Prettier than the usual two-slice sandwich, the open-face variety adds eye appeal to any table. Spread bread slices with butter or mayonnaise and top with:
- *smoked salmon, onion rings and dill sprigs*
- *deviled ham and chilled asparagus spears*
- *rolled slices of Virginia ham filled with chopped pickles*

Herbed Lamb Chops

FLAVOR, ZEST AND COLOR IN A SIMPLE FEAST

A simple wine- and garlic-flavored marinade makes our Herbed Lamb Chops savory and succulent while you prepare a colorful vegetable medley. Poppy seed and coffee liqueur turn good old vanilla ice cream into a tasty dessert surprise.

═══ Menu for 6 ═══

- **Herbed Lamb Chops**
- **Buttered Orzo**
- **Zucchini with Red Pepper and Onion**
- **Poppy Seed Ice Cream and Butter Cookies**

SHOPPING LIST

- ☐ 4 loin lamb chops
- ☐ 2 large zucchini
- ☐ 1 medium onion
- ☐ 1 red pepper
- ☐ 1 bunch fresh oregano (optional)
- ☐ 1 16-ounce package orzo
- ☐ 1 box or package butter cookies
- ☐ 1 jar poppy seed
- ☐ 1 pint vanilla ice cream
- ☐ Coffee-flavored liqueur

Have on Hand
- ☐ Salt
- ☐ Pepper
- ☐ Garlic
- ☐ Oregano

- ☐ Salad oil
- ☐ Olive oil
- ☐ Red wine vinegar
- ☐ Dijon mustard
- ☐ Butter or margarine
- ☐ 1 lemon

SCHEDULE

1. Marinate lamb chops.
2. Prepare Zucchini with Red Pepper and Onion.
3. Cook orzo.
4. Prepare Poppy Seed Ice Cream.
5. Broil lamb chops.

Herbed Lamb Chops

4   loin lamb chops
¼   cup salad oil
2   tablespoons olive oil
2   tablespoons red wine vinegar
1   garlic clove, crushed
1   teaspoon Dijon mustard
2   teaspoons fresh oregano or
      1 teaspoon dried
1   teaspoon salt
⅛   teaspoon pepper
      Lemon slices
      Fresh oregano, for garnish
      (optional)

Place lamb chops in a shallow dish. In jar with tight-fitting lid combine oils, vinegar, garlic, mustard, oregano, salt and pepper. Shake to combine. Pour over chops and marinate 10 to 15 minutes. Preheat broiler. Place chops on broiler rack and baste with marinade. Cook 3 inches from heat 3 to 5 minutes. Baste, then turn, baste again and cook 3 to 5 minutes more. Garnish with lemon slices and sprigs of fresh oregano, if available.

Zucchini with Red Pepper and Onion

2   tablespoons olive oil
1   medium onion, chopped
1   red pepper, chopped
2   garlic cloves, pressed
2   large zucchini, cut into cubes
1   teaspoon salt
⅛   teaspoon pepper

In medium skillet heat oil over medium-high heat. Add onion, red pepper and garlic; saute 5 minutes, stirring occasionally. Add zucchini and continue to saute 10 to 15 minutes, until vegetables are tender. Season with salt and pepper.

Poppy Seed Ice Cream

3   tablespoons coffee-flavored
      liqueur
1   pint vanilla ice cream,
      softened
2   tablespoons poppy seed

Blend liqueur with ice cream. Stir in poppy seed. Divide among 4 dessert dishes. Return to freezer until serving time.

OREGANO FOR FLAVOR AND AROMA

When fresh oregano is available, try adding a sprig to:
• *chilled vegetable juice cocktail*
• *tomato soup*
• *green salads*
• *broiled or poached fish or shellfish*

Use dried oregano to lend flavor interest to:
• *meat stews*
• *chili con carne*
• *stewed chicken*
• *broiled or stewed tomatoes*
• *hamburgers and cheeseburgers*

Stir-Fried Beef and Zucchini

QUICK AND DELICIOUS CHINESE-STYLE STIR-FRY

The people of China use the stir-fry method because it requires very little precious fuel. We cook this way because the method is quick and results in tasty, crisp foods. Most Chinese chefs do their stir-frying in peanut oil.

Menu for 6

Egg Rolls
• Stir-Fried Beef
  and Zucchini
Rice

• Imperial Bean
  Sprout Salad
• Oriental
  Sundaes

SHOPPING LIST

- ☐ 2 pounds round steak
- ☐ 2 medium onions
- ☐ 2 medium zucchini
- ☐ 1/2 pound bean sprouts
- ☐ 1 bunch radishes
- ☐ 1 head Bibb or Boston lettuce
- ☐ 1 jar preserved kumquats
- ☐ 1 package or can chow mein noodles
- ☐ 1 quart orange sherbet
- ☐ 6 prepared or frozen egg rolls

Have on Hand
- ☐ Long-grain rice
- ☐ Sugar
- ☐ Cornstarch

- ☐ Salt
- ☐ Pepper
- ☐ Garlic
- ☐ Peanut or salad oil
- ☐ Tarragon vinegar
- ☐ Soy sauce
- ☐ Dry white wine

SCHEDULE

1. Prepare egg rolls.
2. Cook rice.
3. Prepare Imperial Bean Sprout Salad.
4. Prepare Stir-Fried Beef and Zucchini.

Stir-Fried Beef and Zucchini

½ cup dry white wine
1 tablespoon cornstarch
1 tablespoon soy sauce
¼ teaspoon pepper
4 tablespoons peanut or
    salad oil, divided
2 pounds round steak, sliced
    into thin strips
1 garlic clove, crushed
2 medium onions, cut into
    bite-sized chunks
2 medium zucchini, sliced

In 1-cup measure combine wine, cornstarch, soy sauce and pepper. In skillet or wok heat 2 tablespoons oil; brown half the beef, stirring quickly and constantly. Remove with slotted spoon. Add 1 tablespoon oil and stir-fry remaining beef; remove and set aside. Heat last tablespoon oil and stir-fry garlic, onions and zucchini. Stir cornstarch mixture and add to skillet or wok along with the beef; heat through.

Imperial Bean Sprout Salad

½ cup salad oil
3 tablespoons tarragon vinegar
½ teaspoon salt
⅛ teaspoon pepper
    Pinch sugar
1 head Bibb or Boston let-
    tuce, torn into pieces

1 bunch radishes, sliced
½ pound bean sprouts

In small jar with tight-fitting lid combine oil, vinegar, salt, pepper and sugar; shake well. In medium salad bowl combine lettuce, radish slices and bean sprouts; pour dressing over vegetables and toss well.

Oriental Sundaes

1 quart orange sherbet
12 preserved kumquats, cut
    into wedges
⅓ cup chow mein noodles,
    for garnish

Place a generous scoop of sherbet in each of 6 dessert dishes. Top with kumquat wedges and chow mein noodle pieces.

ZUCCHINI TIPS

- *This quick and interesting zucchini recipe is especially good with pork and fish entrees: Cook sliced zucchini in boiling salted water until tender. Drain; add in about ½ can thawed orange juice concentrate. Heat through.*
- *With soup-and-sandwich meals serve a simple but tasty zucchini salad: Combine lettuce, tomato wedges and small white onion rings with thinly sliced zucchini; toss with bottled Italian or French dressing.*

Red Beans and Rice with Ham, page 48

Beans in Burger Cups, page 50

Micro Meat Loaf, page 52

Acapulco Omelet, page 54

Bacony Chicken Breasts, page 56   *Glazed Ham Steaks, page 58*

Red Beans and Rice with Ham

COLORFUL NEW VERSION OF AN OLD FAVORITE

Hearty, protein-packed Red Beans and Rice with Ham is a pleasing entree for a chilly evening.

Menu for 4

- **Red Beans and Rice with Ham**
- **Garlicky Parmesan Bread**
- **Fried Okra**
- **Coconut-Pecan Angel Cake**

SHOPPING LIST

- ☐ 1 pound cooked ham
- ☐ 1 pound fresh okra or 2 10-ounce packages whole frozen okra
- ☐ 1 large onion
- ☐ 1 bunch celery
- ☐ 1 16-ounce can red kidney beans
- ☐ 1 small can or package chopped pecans
- ☐ 1 small can or package shredded coconut
- ☐ 1 angel food cake
- ☐ 1 loaf French bread
- ☐ 1 8-ounce container whipped topping made with real cream

- ☐ Salt
- ☐ Thyme
- ☐ Basil
- ☐ Red pepper sauce
- ☐ Garlic
- ☐ Salad oil
- ☐ Prepared salad dressing
- ☐ Butter or margarine
- ☐ Parmesan cheese

Have on Hand
- ☐ Long-grain rice
- ☐ Brown sugar

SCHEDULE

1. Prepare Red Beans and Rice with Ham.
2. Prepare fried okra.
3. Prepare topping for Coconut-Pecan Angel Cake.
4. Prepare Garlicky Parmesan Bread.

Red Beans and Rice with Ham

2	*tablespoons salad oil*
1	*cup chopped onions*
1/2	*cup chopped celery*
2	*garlic cloves, minced*
1	*can (16 oz.) red kidney beans*
2	*cups cubed cooked ham*
1/2	*cup long-grain rice*
1	*teaspoon salt*
1/2	*teaspoon red pepper sauce*
1/4	*teaspoon freshly ground pepper*
1/4	*teaspoon thyme*
1/4	*teaspoon basil*

In 3-quart saucepan heat oil. Add onions, celery and garlic; saute until onions are translucent. Drain beans; reserve liquid. Add enough water to liquid to measure 3 cups. Add liquid and remaining ingredients to saucepan and bring to a boil. Reduce heat; cover and simmer 20 minutes.

Garlicky Parmesan Bread

1/4	*cup butter or margarine*
2	*tablespoons minced garlic*
1	*loaf crusty French bread, sliced into 10 to 13 pieces*
2	*tablespoons grated Parmesan cheese*

Preheat oven to 350° F. In small saucepan melt butter or margarine; stir in garlic and saute 5 minutes. Brush on both sides of bread slices. Place bread in baking pan; sprinkle cheese on top. Heat in oven 10 minutes.

Coconut-Pecan Angel Cake

2	*tablespoons butter or margarine*
2/3	*cup shredded coconut*
1/2	*cup chopped pecans*
2/3	*cup brown sugar*
1/2	*cup water*
4	*thick slices angel food cake*
1/2	*cup whipped topping made with real cream*

In medium saucepan melt butter or margarine over medium heat. Add coconut and pecans. Cook, stirring, until coconut is golden brown, about 5 minutes. Add brown sugar and water. Bring to a boil; boil 2 minutes. Set aside to cool slightly.

In each of 4 dessert dishes place 1 slice cake; spoon on coconut-pecan mixture and top with whipped topping.

PERFECT FRIED OKRA

In medium bowl combine 3/4 cup cornmeal, 1/3 cup all-purpose flour, 1 teaspoon salt and 1/8 teaspoon pepper. Add 1 pound sliced okra or 2 packages (10 oz. each) whole frozen okra; toss well. In 10-inch skillet heat enough bacon drippings, butter or margarine to cover bottom of pan. Add okra and cook, turning often, until crisp and browned. Drain on paper towels.

Bean 'n' Burger Cups

NEW PRESENTATION OF AN OLD FAVORITE

Here's a hurry-up meal that features everybody's favorite foods—hamburgers, baked beans, tomatoes and chips. Our Confetti Cole Slaw is extra creamy.

Menu for 4

- **Bean 'n' Burger Cups**
- **Confetti Cole Slaw**

Potato Chips
Cherry Tomatoes
- **Cocoa Banana Smoothies**

SHOPPING LIST

- ☐ 1 pound carrots
- ☐ 1 pint cherry tomatoes
- ☐ 1 head cabbage (1 pound)
- ☐ 1 medium onion
- ☐ 1 bunch green onions
- ☐ 2 ripe bananas
- ☐ 1 16-ounce can pork and beans in tomato sauce
- ☐ 1 package chocolate sandwich cookies
- ☐ 1 bag potato chips
- ☐ 1 8-ounce container sour cream
- ☐ 1 8-ounce container frozen whipped topping made with real cream
- ☐ 1 pound ground beef

Have on Hand
- ☐ Bacon
- ☐ Sugar
- ☐ Brown sugar
- ☐ Unsweetened cocoa or cocoa mix
- ☐ Salt
- ☐ Dry mustard
- ☐ Red pepper sauce
- ☐ Steak sauce
- ☐ Ketchup
- ☐ Mayonnaise
- ☐ Eggs
- ☐ 1 lemon
- ☐ Bread crumbs
- ☐ Milk

SCHEDULE

1. Prepare Cocoa Banana Smoothies.
2. Prepare Confetti Cole Slaw.
3. Prepare Bean 'n' Burger Cups.

Bean 'n' Burger Cups

1   pound ground beef
¼   cup unseasoned bread crumbs
½   cup chopped green onions, divided
¼   cup milk
2   tablespoons bottled steak sauce
1   egg, beaten
½   teaspoon salt
4   slices bacon
1   onion, chopped
1   can (16 oz.) pork and beans in tomato sauce
¼   cup ketchup
1   tablespoon brown sugar
1   teaspoon dry mustard
    Dash red pepper sauce

Preheat oven to 375° F. In medium bowl combine ground beef, bread crumbs, ¼ cup green onions, milk, steak sauce, beaten egg and salt; mix well. Divide mixture among 4 greased 10-ounce glass custard cups, patting against bottom and sides. Place cups on cookie sheet; bake 10 minutes. Pour off drippings.

Meanwhile, in skillet cook bacon until crisp; drain on paper towels and crumble. Pour off all but 1 tablespoon bacon drippings. Add chopped onion and saute until translucent. Add pork and beans, ketchup, brown sugar, dry mustard and red pepper sauce; stir to combine. Cook until heated through.

Remove meat cups from custard cups. Spoon beans evenly into each; garnish with crumbled bacon and remaining ¼ cup chopped green onions.

Confetti Cole Slaw

1   medium carrot
3   green onions
1   pound cabbage, cut into chunks
½   cup sour cream
½   cup mayonnaise
    Juice of ½ lemon
1   teaspoon sugar
½   teaspoon salt
    Dash red pepper sauce

In food processor shred carrot. Shred green onions and cabbage chunks. Transfer mixture to large bowl. To processor fitted with steel blade add sour cream, mayonnaise, lemon juice, sugar, salt and red pepper sauce. Process until well mixed. Toss dressing with vegetables.

Cocoa Banana Smoothies

1   tablespoon unsweetened cocoa or 2 tablespoons cocoa mix
1   cup frozen whipped topping with real cream, thawed
2   ripe bananas, sliced
8   chocolate sandwich cookies, crumbled

In medium bowl stir cocoa or cocoa mix into whipped topping. Fold in sliced bananas and half the crumbled cookies. Divide into four serving dishes; garnish with remaining cookies. Refrigerate until serving time.

Micro Meat Loaf

DELICIOUS MEAT LOAF—EASY AS 1-2-3

We've come a long way since the days when it took over an hour to prepare a meat loaf. This one cooks in the microwave while you prepare the vegetables— a total of fourteen minutes' cooking time.

Menu for 4

- **Micro Meat Loaf**
  Instant Mashed Potatoes with Chives
- **Green Beans with Mushrooms**
- **Lime Dream Pie**

SHOPPING LIST

- ☐ 1 pound fresh green beans
- ☐ ¼ pound fresh mushrooms
- ☐ 1 bunch chives
- ☐ 1 lime
- ☐ 1 9-inch chocolate-flavored pie crust
- ☐ 1 package onion soup mix
- ☐ 1 package herb-seasoned stuffing mix
- ☐ 1 8-ounce container frozen whipped topping made with real cream
- ☐ 1 6-ounce can frozen limeade
- ☐ 1 pound ground beef

Have on Hand
- ☐ Brown sugar

- ☐ Salt
- ☐ Garlic
- ☐ Dijon-style mustard
- ☐ Butter or margarine
- ☐ Ketchup
- ☐ Instant mashed potatoes
- ☐ Green food coloring (optional)

SCHEDULE

1. Prepare Lime Dream Pie.
2. Prepare Micro Meat Loaf.
3. Prepare Green Beans with Mushrooms.
4. Prepare instant mashed potatoes with chives.

Micro Meat Loaf

1 pound ground beef
¼ cup onion soup mix
1 cup water
½ cup herb-seasoned stuffing mix
⅓ cup ketchup
3 tablespoons brown sugar
1½ teaspoons Dijon-style mustard

In medium bowl combine ground beef, soup mix, water and stuffing mix; blend well. Press into an 8 x 4-inch microwave-proof dish. Top with wax paper. Microwave on High 10 minutes, rotating dish once. Drain off juices. Combine ketchup, brown sugar and mustard. Spoon over meat loaf. Microwave uncovered 3 to 4 minutes or until loaf is cooked in center (test with knife). Let stand a few minutes before serving.

Green Beans with Mushrooms

1 pound fresh green beans, trimmed
¾ teaspoon salt
3 tablespoons butter or margarine
1 small garlic clove, minced
1 cup sliced mushrooms

In large saucepan cook beans with salt in boiling water to cover 10 to 12 minutes until tender-crisp. Meanwhile, in medium skillet melt butter or margarine; add garlic and saute over low heat 5 minutes until tender. Add mushrooms to skillet and saute over medium heat, stirring occasionally until tender and slightly browned. Drain beans well; place in serving bowl and toss with mushrooms and garlic butter.

Lime Dream Pie

2 containers (8 oz. each) frozen whipped topping made with real cream
1 can (6 oz.) frozen limeade Peel of 1 lime, grated
4 drops green food coloring (optional)
1 prepared 9-inch chocolate-flavored pie crust

In mixer bowl combine frozen whipped topping, limeade, lime peel and food coloring. Spoon into prepared crust. Refrigerate or freeze until serving time.

COVERING FOODS DURING MICROWAVING

- *To seal in moisture and aid in steaming and tenderizing, cover food with lid, dinner plate or plastic wrap, turned back at the corner.*
- *Covering a dish with wax paper helps to equalize the cooking of unevenly shaped foods such as chicken parts; place the wax paper loosely on top of the dish.*
- *Use paper towels when you want the cover to absorb some of the moisture in the foods; bacon cooked between two paper towels will be dry and crisp.*

Acapulco Omelets

OMELET MEAL WITH A MEXICAN FLAIR

Jalapeño peppers establish the Mexican theme of this omelet meal. Serve the tropical salad plain or with one of the dressings offered in the Tips. Jerusalem artichokes, sometimes called sunchokes, will do very well if you can't find jicama.

Menu for 4

- ### Acapulco Omelets Warmed Corn Tortillas

- ### Jicama-Avocado Salad
- ### Sombrero Sundaes

SHOPPING LIST

- ☐ 1   small onion
- ☐ 3   medium tomatoes
- ☐ 1   jicama
- ☐ 1   avocado
- ☐ 1   head leafy lettuce
- ☐ 2-3   jalapeño peppers, fresh or canned
- ☐ 1   package corn tortillas
- ☐ 1   8-ounce bottle lime juice or 6 limes
- ☐ ½   pint heavy or whipping cream
- ☐ 1   4-ounce package shredded Cheddar cheese
- ☐ 1   quart coffee ice cream
- ☐   Coffee bean candies
- ☐   Aromatic bitters
- ☐   Coffee liqueur

Have on Hand
- ☐   Sugar
- ☐   Salt
- ☐   Pepper
- ☐   Salad oil
- ☐   Eggs
- ☐   Butter or margarine

SCHEDULE

1. Prepare Jicama-Avocado Salad.
2. Warm tortillas in slow oven.
3. Prepare Acapulco Omelets.

Acapulco Omelets

1   tablespoon salad oil
½   cup chopped onion
3   medium tomatoes,
      chopped
2   or 3 fresh or canned
      jalapeño peppers,
      seeded and minced
6   eggs
1   tablespoon water
¼   teaspoon salt
      Dash pepper
4   tablespoons butter or
      margarine,
      divided
½   cup (2 oz.) shredded
      Cheddar cheese,
      divided

In heavy skillet heat oil over medium heat. Add onion and saute until translucent. Add tomatoes and peppers. Cook, stirring occasionally, 10 minutes; set aside.

In medium bowl combine eggs, water, salt and pepper. Beat lightly with a fork. In skillet or omelet pan melt 2 tablespoons butter or margarine over medium heat. When butter bubbles, pour in *half* the egg mixture. Shake the pan gently and stir for a few seconds. Then let eggs settle, lifting the cooked part to let the loose egg run underneath. While eggs are still quite soft, sprinkle shredded cheese over top and cook 1 more minute. Fold one-third of omelet over; slide onto warm serving plate. Repeat with remaining butter, eggs and cheese. Serve omelets with tomato-pepper sauce.

Jicama-Avocado Salad

⅓   cup lime juice
1   teaspoon sugar
¼   teaspoon aromatic bitters
      Dash salt
1   jicama, thinly sliced
1   avocado, cut into chunks
4   large lettuce leaves

In measuring cup combine lime juice, sugar, bitters and salt; stir well with fork. In medium bowl toss jicama and avocado with dressing. Mound on lettuce leaves.

Sombrero Sundaes

1   quart coffee ice cream
¾   cup coffee liqueur
½   cup heavy or whipping
      cream, whipped
      Coffee bean candies (optional)

Place 2 scoops ice cream in each dish and pour on about 3 tablespoons coffee liqueur. Top each serving with a dollop of whipped cream and coffee bean candy.

TROPICAL FRUIT SALAD DRESSINGS

- *Summer Lime Dressing:* ½ cup fresh lime juice, ½ cup water, 1 tablespoon sugar and dash salt
- *Tangy Cream Dressing:* 3 tablespoons half and half cream, 1 tablespoon cider vinegar, 2 teaspoons sugar, ¼ teaspoon salt

Bacony Chicken Breasts

CHICKEN BREASTS—FAST AND FLAVORFUL

Canned mushrooms and potatoes help beat the clock here. The fresher and tinier the asparagus, the faster it will cook, and the more delicious it will taste.

Menu for 4

- **Bacony Chicken Breasts Steamed Asparagus with Dill Butter**

- **Three-Pepper Salad Strawberries with Sour Cream**

SHOPPING LIST

- ☐ 4 chicken cutlets
- ☐ 1 pound bacon
- ☐ 1 pound fresh asparagus
- ☐ 1 head leaf lettuce
- ☐ 1 green pepper
- ☐ 1 red pepper
- ☐ 1 yellow pepper
- ☐ 1 small onion
- ☐ 1 small red onion
- ☐ 1 bunch fresh dill or dillweed
- ☐ 1 pint strawberries or 1 12-ounce package frozen strawberries
- ☐ 1 6-ounce can sliced mushrooms
- ☐ 1 16-ounce can whole new potatoes
- ☐ 1 8-ounce container sour cream

Have on Hand
- ☐ Salt
- ☐ Pepper
- ☐ Garlic
- ☐ Salad oil
- ☐ Olive oil
- ☐ Red wine vinegar
- ☐ Butter or margarine

SCHEDULE

1. Prepare Bacony Chicken Breasts.
2. Prepare Steamed Asparagus with Dill Butter.
3. Prepare Three-Pepper Salad.

Bacony Chicken Breasts

1   can (16 oz.) whole new
       potatoes, drained
1   can (6 oz.) sliced mush-
       rooms, drained
½   teaspoon salt
4   slices bacon, quartered
2   tablespoons butter or
       margarine
1   tablespoon salad oil
4   chicken cutlets

Preheat broiler. Slice potatoes ½ inch
thick; pat dry with paper towel. Arrange
in bottom of 13 x 9-inch broiler pan.
Cover with mushrooms, sprinkle with salt
and top with bacon slices. Broil 10 minutes, turning occasionally.

Meanwhile in heavy skillet melt butter
or margarine with oil over medium-high
heat. Saute chicken 2 to 3 minutes on each
side. Transfer to serving plate. Top with
broiled potatoes, mushrooms and bacon.

Three-Pepper Salad

2   tablespoons red wine
       vinegar
1   small garlic clove, pressed
¼   teaspoon salt

⅛   teaspoon pepper
¼   cup olive oil
4   large well-shaped lettuce
       leaves
1   green pepper, cut into
       1-inch pieces
1   sweet red pepper, cut into
       1-inch pieces
1   yellow pepper, cut into
       1-inch pieces
1   small red onion, sliced and
       separated into rings

In small jar with tight-fitting lid combine
vinegar, garlic, salt, pepper and oil; shake
well. On each of 4 salad plates place 1
lettuce leaf; arrange on each one-fourth
of the pepper chunks and red onion rings.
Shake dressing; drizzle over salads.

BROILED CHICKEN KABOBS

*For a tasty appetizer or party snack,
cut chicken cutlets into 1-inch pieces.
Thread on short skewers; season with
salt, pepper and paprika. Brush with
melted butter or margarine and broil
5 inches from heat about 3 to 4 minutes on each side, basting occasionally. For variety and color, skewer
chicken pieces alternately with one of
the following:*
- *cherry tomatoes*
- *parboiled green pepper chunks*
- *whole mushrooms*
- *pineapple chunks*
- *canned sweet potatoes*
- *partly cooked bacon squares*

Glazed Ham Steak

HAM STEAK WITH AN ELEGANT LOOK

Even the fussiest eaters usually like ham, so this steak, with its apple-flavored glaze, should be a hit. Brighten up fresh Brussels sprouts with cherry tomatoes. The smooth blender dessert can be made with fruit other than pears, if desired.

Menu for 6

- **Glazed Ham Steak**
- **Corn Muffins**
- **Brussels Sprouts with Cherry Tomatoes**
- **Pear Parfaits**

SHOPPING LIST

- ☐ 1 ham steak, about 1 inch thick (1½ pounds)
- ☐ 2 10-ounce containers Brussels sprouts
- ☐ 1 pint cherry tomatoes
- ☐ 1 bunch fresh basil (optional)
- ☐ 1 16-ounce can pear halves
- ☐ 1 quart apple juice
- ☐ 1 package corn muffins or 1 box corn bread mix
- ☐ 1 8-ounce container sour cream

Have on Hand
- ☐ Cornstarch
- ☐ Sugar
- ☐ Brown sugar

- ☐ Salt
- ☐ Pepper
- ☐ Ginger
- ☐ Nutmeg
- ☐ 1 lemon or lemon juice
- ☐ Cider vinegar
- ☐ Butter or margarine
- ☐ Dijon-style mustard
- ☐ Raisins

SCHEDULE

1. Prepare Pear Parfaits; chill.
2. Prepare Glazed Ham Steak.
3. Prepare Brussels Sprouts with Cherry Tomatoes.

Glazed Ham Steak

1 **ham steak, about 1 inch
   thick (1½ lbs.)**
3 **cups apple juice, divided**
½ **cup raisins**
½ **cup firmly packed brown sugar**
1 **tablespoon cornstarch**
2 **tablespoons cider vinegar**
1 **teaspoon Dijon mustard**
¼ **teaspoon ginger**

Marinate ham steak in 1 cup apple juice 10 minutes or longer. Drain ham and discard juice. In small saucepan cook raisins in 2 cups apple juice 5 minutes. Add remaining ingredients and cook until thickened.

Preheat broiler. Place ham steak on broiler pan. Brush with sauce. Broil about 4 inches from heat 7 minutes on one side. Turn, brush with sauce and broil 10 minutes. Serve ham with remaining sauce.

Brussels Sprouts with Cherry Tomatoes

2   **containers (10 oz. each)
    Brussels sprouts, trimmed**
½   **teaspoon salt**
3   **tablespoons butter or margarine**
12 **cherry tomatoes, trimmed**
1   **tablespoon chopped fresh
    basil (optional)**
⅛   **teaspoon pepper**

In large saucepan cook Brussels sprouts with salt in boiling water 12 to 15 minutes, just until tender; drain well. Meanwhile, in large skillet melt butter or margarine. Add cherry tomatoes and saute, stirring constantly, until heated through. Add basil to skillet and cook 1 minute. Transfer Brussels sprouts to serving dish; toss with cherry tomatoes and season with pepper.

Pear Parfaits

1   **can (16 oz.) pear halves,
    well drained**
1   **tablespoon lemon juice**
1   **cup sour cream**
1   **tablespoon sugar**
⅛   **teaspoon ground nutmeg**

In blender puree pears with lemon juice until smooth. In small bowl combine sour cream, sugar and nutmeg. Layer pureed pears and flavored sour cream in parfait glasses.

ANOTHER LUSCIOUS PEAR DESSERT

In food processor or blender puree 2 well-drained 16-ounce cans pears in heavy syrup. Stir in 2 tablespoons pear brandy and 1 tablespoon lemon juice; set aside. In small saucepan sprinkle 1 envelope unflavored gelatin over ½ cup milk; let stand 1 minute. Stir over low heat 5 minutes, until gelatin is dissolved; stir in ⅓ cup confectioners' sugar and pear mixture. Chill until serving time. Fold in ½ cup whipped cream; spoon into parfait glasses.

Seafood Newburg, page 62

Seafood Newburg

ELEGANT ENTREE—AN ECONOMICAL NEW WAY

This novel Newburg entree is made with surimi—imitation crab legs—which are tasty and economical as well as quick and easy to prepare. We think you'll like our new and different treatment of peas; they pick up flavor from the cucumber chunks and dill-weed. The hot fruit dessert is absolutely yummy.

═══ Menu for 6 ═══

- **Seafood Newburg** • **Dilled Peas and Rice**   **Cucumbers**
  - **Baked Peach-Berry Crunch**

SHOPPING LIST

- ☐ 1 pound surimi (imitation crab legs)
- ☐ ¼ pound mushrooms
- ☐ 1 green or red pepper
- ☐ 1 small cucumber
- ☐ 1 package amaretto cookies
- ☐ 1 10-ounce package frozen peas
- ☐ 1 10-ounce package frozen raspberries
- ☐ 1 20-ounce package frozen sliced peaches
- ☐ 1 pint vanilla ice cream

Have on Hand
- ☐ Flour

- ☐ Long-grain rice
- ☐ Salt
- ☐ Dillweed
- ☐ Butter or margarine
- ☐ Dry sherry
- ☐ Milk

SCHEDULE

1. Cook rice.
2. Prepare Dilled Peas and Cucumbers.
3. Prepare Baked Peach-Berry Crunch.
4. Prepare Seafood Newburg.

Seafood Newburg

4	tablespoons butter or margarine
1	green or red pepper, seeded and coarsely chopped
¼	pound mushrooms, sliced
2	tablespoons flour
1½	cups milk
3	tablespoons dry sherry
¼	teaspoon salt
1	pound surimi (imitation crab legs), thawed if frozen, cut diagonally into 1-inch pieces

In large skillet melt butter or margarine over medium heat. Add chopped pepper and sliced mushrooms; saute about 5 minutes. Stir in flour and cook 1 minute, stirring constantly. Add milk and continue stirring until sauce is smooth and thickened. Add sherry and salt. Stir in surimi; simmer just until heated through, 2 to 3 minutes.

Dilled Peas and Cucumbers

1	package (10 oz.) frozen peas
1	tablespoon butter or margarine
1	small cucumber, peeled, seeded and cut into ½-inch pieces
¼	teaspoon dillweed

In small saucepan cook peas according to package directions; drain. Meanwhile, in medium skillet melt butter or margarine. Add cucumber and dillweed; saute 1 minute. Add peas to cucumber; toss to mix and heat through.

Baked Peach-Berry Crunch

1	package (10 oz.) frozen raspberries
1	package (20 oz.) frozen sliced peaches
8	amaretto cookies
2	tablespoons butter or margarine
1	pint vanilla ice cream

Preheat oven to 400° F. In small saucepan heat frozen raspberries until melted. Meanwhile, spread frozen sliced peaches in single layer in a 13 x 9-inch baking dish. Pour hot raspberries over peaches. With a rolling pin crush amaretto cookies to make about ⅔ cup crumbs. Sprinkle over fruit. Dot with butter or margarine. Bake 15 minutes. Serve topped with vanilla ice cream.

EXTRA SPECIAL PEACH DESSERT

Named after Dame Nellie Melba, the famous Australian soprano, Peach Melba is one of the most beautiful and delicious of all ice cream desserts. Place 1 peeled and pitted fresh peach half in each dessert bowl. Slide 1 scoop vanilla ice cream in beside it. Drizzle raspberry puree (Melba sauce) over it and top with whipped cream.

A Cheese Ball for All Occasions

Let a 5-ounce jar of Old English cheese, a 4-ounce package of blue cheese and an 8-ounce package of cream cheese come to room temperature. In large bowl combine cheeses and add 1 tablespoon Worcestershire sauce, ⅛ teaspoon garlic powder, ⅛ teaspoon bottled red pepper sauce, ¼ teaspoon salt and red pepper to taste. Blend thoroughly with hands. Divide cheese mixture into two portions and shape into balls. Roll each ball in a mixture of 1 cup chopped pecans and 1 cup chopped parsley.

Quick Tricks with Sweet Potatoes

Start with a can of sweet potatoes and whip up:
- Cran-Sweets: *In medium skillet melt butter or margarine; stir in cranberry-orange relish and chopped pecans to taste. Add sweet potatoes (sliced, if you like); cover and heat. Garnish with orange slices.*
- Sweet-Bake: *Preheat oven to 350° F. In a casserole layer sliced sweet potatoes alternately with sliced apples. Sprinkle with brown sugar, dot with butter, and dust with grated lemon peel to taste. Bake until apple slices are tender.*
- Garden Trio: *In large skillet melt small amount of butter or margarine; add sliced sweet potatoes and heat. Add equal amounts of cooked carrots and butternut squash; season with honey, orange juice, and a little grated orange peel.*
- Mock Pumpkin: *Mash drained sweet potatoes and substitute for pumpkin in bread or pie recipes.*

Fish 'n' Slaw Sandwiches

Prepare 12 ounces of frozen breaded fish fillets (4 portions) according to package directions. Split and toast 4 sesame-seed-topped hamburger rolls. Top each hot fillet with a slice of pasteurized process cheese immediately after removing from oven. Place fillets on bottom halves of rolls; spoon ¼ cup deli cole slaw over each fillet and cover with remaining halves of rolls.

Super Cherry Tomato Snacks

- *Spread thin-sliced party size rye bread with Russian dressing, top with small salami slices and halved cherry tomatoes.*
- *Slice off tomato tops and squeeze gently to remove seeds and pulp. Fill with a mixture of softened cream cheese and horseradish to taste.*

Thyme Tips

- *The taste of thyme is often described as refreshingly mint-like. Thyme comes in many varieties, including lemon, orange and caraway thyme.*
- *Thyme is one of the strongest of seasonings; use it sparingly, a few leaves at a time, in chowders, gumbos, pâtés, bouquet garni.*

Pie Perfection

Weighting down the pastry will keep a single-crust pie shell from buckling and blistering. When it's ready for baking, line with foil and fill with dried beans, uncooked rice or aluminum pie weights. Remove foil and contents 15 minutes after putting pie shell in oven. Bake crust 5 minutes more until golden. Beans, or other weights, can be reused.

Ham Spread in a Hurry

Using your food processor to grind the ham for this recipe will make it even quicker to fix. In medium bowl combine 1½ cups ground ham, 2 tablespoons Dijon mustard, 2 tablespoons finely chopped drained chutney, and 1 tablespoon minced onion. Stir in enough sour cream to bind—about 3 to 4 tablespoons. Use as a sandwich filling or, to serve as an appetizer, mound on cucumber slices, spoon into hollowed-out cherry tomatoes, or spread on cocktail bread slices. Makes about 1¾ cups.

Open-Face Cheese Sandwiches

HEARTY SANDWICHES WITH A WHOLESOME SOUP

Use Jarlsberg cheese to make these hot protein-rich sandwiches. The garlicky Spinach-Potato Soup and the fruit-and-ginger dessert are sure to become stand-bys for quick meals.

Menu for 4

- **Spinach-Potato Soup**
- **Broiled Open-Face Jarlsberg Cheese Sandwiches**
- **Carrot and Celery Sticks**
- **Hot Gingered Pineapple Sundaes**

SHOPPING LIST

- ☐ ½ pound Jarlsberg cheese
- ☐ ¾ pound all-purpose potatoes
- ☐ ½ pound fresh spinach
- ☐ 1 large tomato
- ☐ 1 pound carrots
- ☐ 1 bunch celery
- ☐ 1 small piece fresh ginger or 1 small jar candied ginger
- ☐ 1 13¾- or 14½-ounce can chicken broth
- ☐ 1 8¼-ounce can crushed pineapple in own juice
- ☐ 1 loaf sliced rye or whole wheat bread
- ☐ 1 pint pineapple sherbet

Have on Hand

- ☐ Salt
- ☐ Pepper
- ☐ Garlic
- ☐ Olive oil
- ☐ Dijon mustard
- ☐ Butter or margarine

SCHEDULE

1. Prepare Spinach-Potato Soup.
2. Prepare carrot and celery sticks.
3. Prepare Broiled Open-Face Jarlsberg Cheese Sandwiches.
4. Prepare Gingered Pineapple Sundaes.

Spinach-Potato Soup

1	tablespoon olive oil
4	garlic cloves, peeled
1	can (13¾ or 14½ oz.) chicken broth
1	cup water
¼	teaspoon salt
	Dash pepper
¾	pound all-purpose potatoes, peeled and cut into ½-inch cubes (about 3 cups)
½	pound fresh spinach leaves

In 4-quart Dutch oven or saucepot heat oil. Add garlic and cook covered over low heat 5 minutes. Add broth, water, salt and pepper. Bring to a boil and simmer 5 minutes. Remove garlic and mash with fork; return to broth. Add potatoes and cook covered 15 minutes. Add spinach and cook 2 to 3 minutes more.

Broiled Open-Face Jarlsberg Cheese Sandwiches

4	slices rye or whole wheat bread
1	tablespoon butter or margarine
4	teaspoons Dijon mustard
½	pound Jarlsberg cheese, sliced
4	slices tomato

Preheat broiler. Lightly toast the bread; spread one side of each slice with butter or margarine and the other side with mustard. Place butter side down on cookie sheet. Place 2 slices of cheese and 1 slice of tomato on bread and broil about 4 inches from heat for 3 to 5 minutes, until cheese is melted.

Hot Gingered Pineapple Sundaes

1	can (8 ¼ oz.) crushed pineapple in own juice
¼	teaspoon grated fresh ginger or chopped candied ginger
1	pint pineapple sherbet

In small saucepan combine crushed pineapple and juice with grated ginger. Bring to a boil and cook 5 minutes. In each of 4 dessert dishes place 1 scoop pineapple sherbet. Top with 2 tablespoons warm sauce.

BROILED CHEESE SANDWICH TIPS

Give a new twist to open-face grilled or broiled cheese sandwiches by topping them with:
- *flat anchovy fillets*
- *cooked broccoli or asparagus spears*
- *cooked whole green beans*
- *pimiento strips and drained capers*
- *thinly sliced pepperoni*
- *cubed cooked ham*
- *thinly sliced green pepper*
- *avocado chunks and bean sprouts*

Chinese Chicken with Peppers and Onions

COLORFUL ORIENTAL FLAVOR CHICKEN ENTREE

Made entirely with fresh ingredients, this menu offers a tasty combination of ginger-flavored chicken and lemony broccoli. The Cantonese appetizer is a delicious opener for almost any dinner.

Menu for 4

- **Cantonese Mushrooms**
- **Chinese Chicken with Peppers and Onions**
Rice

- **Steamed Broccoli with Lemon Zest**
Honeydew Melon

SHOPPING LIST

- ☐ 4 chicken cutlets
- ☐ 1 bunch broccoli (about 1½ pounds)
- ☐ 1 bunch green onions
- ☐ 16 large mushrooms
- ☐ 2 medium green peppers
- ☐ 2 small hot red peppers or crushed red pepper
- ☐ 2 medium onions
- ☐ 1 small piece fresh ginger
- ☐ 1 honeydew melon

Have on Hand
- ☐ Long-grain rice
- ☐ Garlic

- ☐ Salad oil
- ☐ Soy sauce
- ☐ Sesame oil
- ☐ Dry sherry
- ☐ 1 lemon

SCHEDULE

1. Cook rice.
2. Cook Chinese Chicken with Peppers and Onions.
3. Prepare Steamed Broccoli with Lemon Zest.
4. Prepare Cantonese Mushrooms.

Cantonese Mushrooms

3   tablespoons salad oil
1   clove garlic, slightly crushed
16   large mushroom caps
3   green onions, cut into
       1-inch strips
3   tablespoons soy sauce
1   tablespoon dry sherry
2   teaspoons sesame oil

In wok or large skillet heat salad oil over medium heat. Add garlic and mushrooms; stir-fry 3 minutes. Remove garlic and discard. Add green onions to pan and toss to coat with oil. Pour soy sauce and sherry over vegetables; reduce heat and cook 5 to 7 minutes, until mushrooms are tender. Remove mushrooms with slotted spoon and divide among 4 small plates. Sprinkle ½ teaspoon sesame oil over each serving.

Chinese Chicken with Peppers and Onions

¼   cup salad oil, divided
2   slices fresh ginger
2   small hot red peppers or
       ¼ teaspoon crushed red pepper
4   chicken cutlets, cut into
       ½-inch pieces
2   medium onions, thinly sliced
2   medium green peppers, cut
       into 1-inch chunks
3   tablespoons soy sauce
¾   teaspoon sesame oil

In wok or large skillet heat 2 tablespoons salad oil until it begins to smoke. Add ginger, hot red peppers or crushed red pepper and chicken; stir-fry until chicken is thoroughly cooked, about 3 minutes. Transfer to serving dish.

Add remaining 2 tablespoons oil to wok and heat. Add onions and green peppers. Stir-fry until onions are translucent. Return chicken to wok; add soy sauce. Stir-fry 1 minute. Sprinkle with sesame oil.

Steamed Broccoli with Lemon Zest

1   bunch (about 1½ lbs.) broccoli
1   teaspoon freshly grated
       lemon peel

Discard broccoli leaves. If stalks are thick, peel off tough outer skin and cut off ends. Remove broccoli florets and reserve. Cut stalks into ¼-inch slices. In large saucepan or skillet bring 1 inch water to a boil. Place broccoli florets and slices in steamer basket and set in boiling water. Cover and steam about 5 minutes until tender-crisp but still bright green. Transfer broccoli to serving dish and toss with lemon zest.

MELON TIPS

• *For dessert or a snack, cut cantaloupe into rings; fill with yogurt and top with granola.*
• *For a tasty low-calorie dessert, roll melon balls in toasted shredded coconut.*

Broiled Lamb Chops

A QUICK AND SATISFYING FAVORITE

Tender lamb chops taste delicious when seasoned with salt and pepper and broiled quickly. Curried Rice and Glazed Carrots make this a special meal.

Menu for 4

Broiled Lamb Chops
• **Curried Rice**
• **Glazed Carrots**

• **Tossed Salad with Tangy Dressing**
• **Angel Fudge Cake**

SHOPPING LIST

- ☐ 4 to 8 loin or shoulder lamb chops, depending on size
- ☐ 1 pound carrots
- ☐ 2 onions
- ☐ 1 head leaf lettuce
- ☐ 1 angel food cake
- ☐ 1 12-ounce jar chocolate fudge topping
- ☐ 1 8-ounce container whipped topping made with real cream
- ☐ 1 pint chocolate or vanilla ice cream

Have on Hand
- ☐ Long-grain rice
- ☐ Sugar
- ☐ Brown sugar
- ☐ Salt

- ☐ Pepper
- ☐ Curry powder
- ☐ Dry mustard
- ☐ Paprika
- ☐ Cider vinegar
- ☐ Salad oil
- ☐ Worcestershire sauce
- ☐ Butter or margarine

SCHEDULE

1. Prepare Curried Rice.
2. Prepare Glazed Carrots.
3. Prepare Tossed Salad with Tangy Dressing.
4. Broil lamb chops.
5. Prepare Angel Fudge Cake.

Curried Rice

1   *cup long-grain rice*
1½ *teaspoons butter or*
      margarine
1   *medium onion, chopped*
1   *teaspoon curry powder*

Cook rice according to package directions. In small skillet heat butter or margarine over medium heat. Add chopped onion and curry powder; cook about 5 minutes or until onion is translucent. Stir in rice; heat through.

Glazed Carrots

1   *pound carrots, peeled and*
      cut into ½-inch pieces
½ *teaspoon salt*
2   *tablespoons butter or*
      margarine
¼ *cup brown sugar*

In medium saucepan cook carrots with salt in water to cover 15 to 20 minutes, until tender; drain and remove carrots. In same saucepan melt butter or margarine; slowly add brown sugar. Return carrots to pan, stirring to coat; cook until heated through.

Tossed Salad with Tangy Dressing

3   *tablespoons cider vinegar*
½ *cup salad oil*
    Dash sugar

1½ *teaspoons Worcestershire*
      sauce
½ *teaspoon dry mustard*
½ *teaspoon paprika*
½ *teaspoon salt*
¼ *teaspoon pepper*
1   *head leaf lettuce, torn*
      into pieces

In small jar with tight-fitting lid combine all ingredients except lettuce; shake well. Pour over lettuce and toss.

Angel Fudge Cake

1   *jar (12 oz.) chocolate fudge*
      topping
4   *slices angel food cake*
4   *scoops chocolate or vanilla*
      ice cream
1   *cup whipped topping made*
      with real cream

Scoop chocolate fudge topping into top of double boiler; heat over slowly boiling water until hot. In each of 4 dessert bowls place 1 slice angel food cake; top with a scoop of ice cream. Drizzle hot fudge over cake and ice cream; add a dollop of whipped topping.

MIDDLE EASTERN RICE VARIATION

Melt 1 tablespoon butter or margarine. Add ¼ cup slivered blanched almonds; cook 2 to 3 minutes, until nuts begin to brown. Stir in cooked long-grain rice. Then fold in ¼ cup chopped pitted dates. Excellent with fish, chicken or lamb.

Turkey Joes

ECONOMICAL MEAL THE KIDS WILL LOVE

Here is a delicious variation on the ever-popular Sloppy Joe, made with quick-cooking ground turkey. Served with french fries and a crisp salad, it makes a simple but memorable meal.

Menu for 6

- **Turkey Joes**
  French Fries
- **Lemony Romaine Salad**
- **Ebony and Ivory Sundaes**

SHOPPING LIST

- ☐ 1 pound ground turkey
- ☐ 1 green pepper
- ☐ 1 small onion
- ☐ 1 small head romaine
- ☐ 2 tomatoes
- ☐ 1 cucumber
- ☐ 1 small red onion
- ☐ 1 bunch fresh basil or dried basil
- ☐ 1 jar marshmallow creme
- ☐ 1 jar or can chocolate syrup
- ☐ 1 small can or package shredded coconut
- ☐ 1 package chocolate chips
- ☐ 1 package hamburger rolls
- ☐ 1 10-ounce package frozen french fries
- ☐ 1 pint chocolate ice cream
- ☐ 1 pint vanilla ice cream

Have on Hand

- ☐ Sugar
- ☐ Salt
- ☐ Pepper
- ☐ Garlic
- ☐ Ground red pepper
- ☐ 1 lemon or lemon juice
- ☐ Olive oil
- ☐ Chili sauce
- ☐ Bottled barbecue sauce
- ☐ Butter or margarine

SCHEDULE

1. Prepare Turkey Joes.
2. Heat french fries.
3. Prepare Lemony Romaine Salad.
4. Prepare Ebony and Ivory Sundaes.

Turkey Joes

2   *tablespoons butter or margarine*
1   *small onion, chopped*
½   *green pepper, chopped*
1   *small clove garlic, minced*
1   *pound ground fresh turkey*
½   *teaspoon salt*
¼   *teaspoon sugar*
¼   *teaspoon ground red pepper*
⅓   *cup bottled barbecue sauce*
2   *tablespoons chili sauce*
4   *hamburger rolls*

In medium skillet melt butter or margarine over medium-high heat. Add onion, green pepper and garlic; saute until onion is translucent. Crumble in ground turkey and saute 10 minutes. Sprinkle with salt, sugar and red pepper; stir to mix. Stir in barbecue and chili sauces. Reduce heat, cover and simmer 20 minutes. Serve on hamburger rolls.

Lemony Romaine Salad

1   *small head romaine*
2   *tomatoes, sliced*
1   *cucumber, sliced*
1   *small red onion, sliced and divided into rings*
2   *tablespoons lemon juice*
½   *teaspoon salt*
⅛   *teaspoon pepper*
1   *teaspoon chopped fresh basil or ⅛ teaspoon dried*
6   *tablespoons olive oil*

Arrange romaine leaves on salad platter. Arrange tomato, cucumber and onion slices on top in rings. In small cup combine lemon juice, salt, pepper and basil. With a fork beat in olive oil. Pour dressing over salad.

Ebony and Ivory Sundaes

1   *pint chocolate ice cream*
1   *pint vanilla ice cream*
4   *tablespoons marshmallow creme*
4   *tablespoons chocolate chips*
4   *tablespoons chocolate syrup*
4   *tablespoons shredded coconut*

In each of 4 dessert dishes place 1 scoop chocolate and 1 scoop vanilla ice cream. Top chocolate ice cream with marshmallow creme and chocolate chips. Top vanilla ice cream with chocolate syrup and shredded coconut.

MAKE-YOUR-OWN SUNDAES

Set out two or three pints of different-flavored ice cream and offer chocolate syrup, strawberry or raspberry topping, marshmallow creme, butterscotch topping, shredded coconut, chopped nuts, chocolate chips and shredded coconut. Or, if you prefer, offer vanilla ice cream with a choice of dessert liqueurs as toppings.

Curry-in-a-Hurry
INDIAN MENU IN MINUTES

Home-cooked Indian food in less than half an hour? Easy! Serve it with rice and the traditional cucumber salad. Then end the meal with a cool and minty melon dessert. Our Tips section offers more ideas for serving cantaloupe, honeydew and other melons.

Menu for 4

- **Curry-in-a-Hurry Rice**
- **Cucumber-Yogurt Salad**
- **Melon Medley**

SHOPPING LIST

- ☐ 1 green pepper
- ☐ 2 medium cucumbers
- ☐ 1 small cantaloupe
- ☐ 1 small honeydew melon
- ☐ 1 bunch fresh mint or dried mint
- ☐ 1 package golden onion soup mix
- ☐ 1 small jar chutney
- ☐ 1 11-ounce can whole seedless litchi nuts
- ☐ 1 small can or package shredded coconut
- ☐ 1 12-ounce can or bottle ginger ale
- ☐ 1 10-ounce package frozen peas
- ☐ 1 16-ounce package peeled and deveined frozen shrimp
- ☐ 1 8-ounce container plain yogurt
- ☐ Orange-flavored liqueur

Have on Hand
- ☐ Long-grain rice
- ☐ All-purpose flour
- ☐ Sugar
- ☐ Garlic
- ☐ Curry powder
- ☐ Ground red pepper
- ☐ Milk
- ☐ Butter or margarine

SCHEDULE

1. Cook rice.
2. Prepare Cucumber-Yogurt Salad.
3. Prepare Melon Medley.
4. Prepare Curry-in-a-Hurry.

Curry-in-a-Hurry

2 tablespoons butter or
    margarine
¼ cup chopped green pepper
1 tablespoon curry powder
3 tablespoons flour
¼ teaspoon ground red
    pepper
1 cup milk
½ cup water
1 envelope golden onion
    soup mix
1 package (16 oz.) peeled
    and deveined frozen
    shrimp
1 cup frozen peas
⅓ cup chutney

In medium saucepan melt butter or margarine. Add green pepper, curry, flour and ground red pepper. Stir constantly 1 minute. Blend in milk, water and soup mix. Simmer 5 minutes, stirring occasionally. Add shrimp, peas and chutney. Simmer until heated through.

Cucumber-Yogurt Salad

1 cup plain yogurt
1 tablespoon chopped fresh
    mint or 1½ teaspoons
    crushed dried mint
1 teaspoon sugar
1 garlic clove, crushed
2 medium cucumbers

In small bowl combine yogurt, mint, sugar and garlic; refrigerate. Peel cucumbers, halve lengthwise and scoop out

seeds. Cut into ¼-inch slices. Toss with dressing at serving time.

Melon Medley

1 small cantaloupe, cut into
    chunks
⅓ honeydew melon, cut into
    chunks
½ can (11 oz.) whole seedless
    litchi nuts
¼ cup shredded coconut
⅓ cup ginger ale
1 tablespoon orange-flavored
    liqueur

In medium bowl combine all ingredients. Refrigerate until serving time.

YUMMY MELON RECIPES

• *Pour 1 quart lemon-lime soda and 2 tablespoons lemon juice into a shallow pan or two ice cube trays. Freeze until mushy, then place in blender with ½ cup cassis or melon liqueur; blend thoroughly and serve over melon balls or chunks in goblets with sprigs of fresh mint.*

• *Cut 1 honeydew or cantaloupe crosswise into rings. Remove seeds and place each ring on lettuce leaves. Fill centers with fresh fruits or colorful sherbet. Garnish with fresh mint.*

• *Cut honeydew or casaba melon into horizontal rings; remove seeds and fill rings with raspberry or orange sherbet. Fill cantaloupe rings with lime or lemon sherbet.*

Sausage and Pepper Pasta

ITALIAN FAVORITES COULDN'T BE QUICKER

Use fast-cooking capellini (very thin spaghetti) for this sausage and pasta entree, which you can whip up in minutes in your microwave oven. Our dessert makes a cool and beautiful finishing touch.

Menu for 6

- **Sausage and Pepper Pasta**
- **Garlic Bread**
- **Tossed Salad with Italian Dressing**
- **Raspberry Icebergs**

SHOPPING LIST

- ☐ ½ pound sweet Italian sausage
- ☐ ½ pound hot Italian sausage
- ☐ ½ pound capellini or fresh pasta
- ☐ Salad greens
- ☐ 1 green pepper
- ☐ 1 red pepper
- ☐ 1 large onion
- ☐ 1 pint fresh raspberries or 1 12-ounce package frozen raspberries
- ☐ 1 loaf French bread
- ☐ 1 pint raspberry ice
- ☐ Black raspberry liqueur

Have on Hand

- ☐ Salt
- ☐ Pepper
- ☐ Garlic
- ☐ Oregano
- ☐ Italian salad dressing
- ☐ Dry white wine

SCHEDULE

1. Prepare Sausage and Pepper Pasta.
2. Prepare garlic bread.
3. Prepare salad.
4. Prepare Raspberry Icebergs.

Sausage and Pepper Pasta

½ pound sweet Italian
   sausage
½ pound hot Italian
   sausage
½ pound capellini or fresh
   pasta
1 green pepper, sliced
1 red pepper, sliced
1 large onion,
   sliced and
   separated into
   rings
4 garlic cloves,
   minced
½ teaspoon oregano
¼ teaspoon salt
⅛ teaspoon pepper
½ cup dry white wine

Prick sausage all over and place in 11 x 8-inch microwave-proof dish. Cover with plastic wrap; slit small hole in top. Microwave on High 3 minutes.

Meanwhile, cook pasta according to package directions.

Remove sausage from microwave-proof dish and set aside; reserve 2 tablespoons drippings in baking dish. Add sliced vegetables. Combine remaining ingredients and pour over vegetables. Cover with plastic wrap; slit small hole in top. Microwave on High 5 minutes, turning once during cooking. Slice sausage and add to vegetables; stir and cover with plastic wrap. Microwave on High 5 minutes, turning once. Serve over pasta.

Raspberry Icebergs

2 cups fresh or frozen
   raspberries, divided
¼ cup black raspberry
   liqueur
1 pint raspberry ice

In blender puree 1 cup raspberries until smooth; stir in liqueur. In each of 4 dessert dishes place 1 scoop raspberry ice. Top each with ¼ cup whole berries and one fourth of the raspberry puree.

FRUIT PUREES AND SAUCES TO TOP OFF A MEAL

- *Using a blender or a food processor, puree strawberries, blueberries, peaches or nectarines, adding sugar to taste or a few tablespoons of fruit-flavored liqueur. Serve the puree over sherbet or other frozen desserts, angel food cake, pound cake or pear halves.*
- *To make a lemony variation of Raspberry Sauce: Puree 1 pint raspberries and ½ cup sugar in blender or food processor; stir in 1 tablespoon lemon juice.*

Sweet 'n' Sassy Chicken

FANCY UP A DELI CHICKEN FOR A SWEET SURPRISE

Combine a prepared chicken with soy sauce, ginger, water chestnuts and snow peas. Serve it with a sesame-flavored salad and fluffy almond-topped rice for a quick Chinese dinner. Quarter the pineapple lengthwise and serve in its own shell.

=== **Menu for 4** ===

- **Sweet 'n' Sassy Chicken**
- **Rice with Almonds**

- **Cucumber- Green Onion Salad with Dill**

Fresh Pineapple Wedges

SHOPPING LIST

- ☐ 1 roasted chicken (about 2 pounds)
- ☐ 1 bunch green onions
- ☐ 2 medium cucumbers
- ☐ 1 bunch fresh dill or dillweed
- ☐ 1 pineapple
- ☐ 1 8-ounce can sliced water chestnuts
- ☐ 1 small can or package sliced almonds
- ☐ 1 10-ounce package frozen sliced carrots
- ☐ 1 6-ounce package frozen snow peas

Have on Hand
- ☐ Long-grain rice
- ☐ Sugar

- ☐ Salt
- ☐ Pepper
- ☐ Ground ginger
- ☐ White wine vinegar
- ☐ Butter or margarine
- ☐ Soy sauce
- ☐ Sesame oil
- ☐ Orange juice
- ☐ Garlic

SCHEDULE

1. Prepare pineapple.
2. Cook Rice with Almonds.
3. Prepare Cucumber-Green Onion Salad with Dill.
4. Prepare Sweet 'n' Sassy Chicken.

Sweet 'n' Sassy Chicken

1   roasted chicken from deli
       counter (about 2 lbs.)
²⁄₃   cup orange juice
3   tablespoons soy sauce
¹⁄₃   cup sliced green onions
1   garlic clove, pressed
¹⁄₂   teaspoon ground ginger
¹⁄₂   teaspoon salt
¹⁄₄   teaspoon pepper
1   cup frozen sliced carrots
1   package (6 oz.) frozen
       snow peas
1   package (6 oz.) sliced
       water chestnuts, drained

Preheat oven to 250° F. Heat chicken on ovenproof serving platter in oven. In medium saucepan combine orange juice, soy sauce, green onions, garlic, ginger, salt and pepper. Bring to a boil. Add carrots; simmer covered 3 minutes. Add snow peas and water chestnuts; simmer 3 minutes more. Remove chicken from oven; surround with vegetables. Spoon sauce over both.

Rice with Almonds

1   cup long-grain rice
2   tablespoons butter or
       margarine
¹⁄₄   cup sliced almonds

Cook rice according to package directions. Meanwhile, in small skillet melt butter or margarine; add almonds and saute over medium heat, stirring occasionally, 5 to 8 minutes. Transfer rice to serving dish; pour melted butter and almonds on top.

Cucumber-Green Onion Salad with Dill

2   medium cucumbers, peeled,
       halved lengthwise and seeded
2   green onions, cut into
       1-inch lengths
1   tablespoon fresh dill or
       1 teaspoon dillweed
¹⁄₂   teaspoon salt
1   teaspoon sugar
2   tablespoons white wine
       vinegar
1   teaspoon sesame oil

Cut each cucumber half into thirds crosswise and then into lengthwise strips. In medium bowl toss cucumber strips with green onions and dill or dillweed. Sprinkle salt, sugar and vinegar over salad and refrigerate until serving time. Add sesame oil and toss well before serving.

FRIED RICE DELIGHTS

Toss leftover cooked rice with cubed ham or pork, chopped onion, ¹⁄₂ cup leftover peas, green beans, snow peas or other green vegetable. Heat 2 tablespoons salad oil in wok or large skillet; toss in 1 whole peeled garlic clove and cook 1 minute; remove and discard. Add rice mixture and stir-fry 4 to 5 minutes, until heated through.

Fish Fillets with Spinach

ELEGANT FISH QUICK AS A WINK

These fillets are filled with a delectable mixture of spinach, onions and feta cheese in a variation on the Florentine cooking style. For a super-fast meal, pop them into the microwave while you whip together the rest of the meal.

Menu for 4

- **Rolled Fish Fillets Stuffed with Spinach**
- **Orange-Flavored Beets**
  Dinner Rolls

Cheesecake

SHOPPING LIST

- ☐ 4   fish fillets (about 1½ pounds)
- ☐ 1   pound spinach
- ☐ 1   medium onion
- ☐ 1   16-ounce can baby beets or sliced beets
- ☐ 1   8-ounce container fresh bread crumbs
- ☐ 1   package brown-and-serve rolls
- ☐ 2   ounces feta cheese
- ☐   Cheesecake

Have on Hand
- ☐   Sugar
- ☐   Cornstarch

- ☐   Salt
- ☐   Pepper
- ☐   Dillweed
- ☐ 1   lemon or lemon juice
- ☐   Orange juice
- ☐   Eggs
- ☐   Butter or margarine

SCHEDULE

1. Prepare Rolled Fish Fillets Stuffed with Spinach.
2. Heat rolls.
3. Prepare Orange-Flavored Beets.

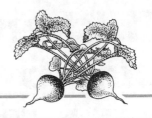

Rolled Fish Fillets Stuffed with Spinach

4	fish fillets (about 1½ lbs.)
3	cups spinach leaves
½	cup chopped onion
¼	cup fresh bread crumbs
2	ounces feta cheese
1	egg
1	tablespoon lemon juice, divided
½	teaspoon salt
½	teaspoon dillweed
⅛	teaspoon pepper

Grease 4 custard cups. Line sides of custard cups with fish, leaving space in center. In food processor with steel blade, combine spinach, onion, bread crumbs, cheese, egg, 2 teaspoons lemon juice and seasonings. Process until smooth. Divide evenly and fill center of each custard cup. Sprinkle remaining 1 teaspoon lemon juice evenly over fish. Place custard cups evenly spaced on round microwave-proof plate. Cover with paper towel. Microwave on High 2 minutes. Turn plate one quarter and continue microwaving 2 to 3 minutes.

Orange-Flavored Beets

1½	teaspoons cornstarch
2½	teaspoons sugar
½	cup orange juice
2	tablespoons butter or margarine
1	can (16 oz.) baby beets or sliced beets, drained

In small saucepan combine cornstarch and sugar; add orange juice slowly, stirring constantly. Cook over medium heat until mixture begins to bubble; lower heat and cook, stirring, until liquid thickens. Add butter or margarine and drained beets; heat through.

COOL AND TASTY BEET SALADS

For color, ease and flavor, serve beet salads on lettuce leaves. Use sliced or baby beets, or pickled beets, artfully arranged with:

- *bean or alfalfa sprouts*
- *white onion rings*
- *shredded green onions*
- *sliced celery*
- *orange slices and grated orange peel*
- *pineapple chunks*
- *jicama slices*
- *avocado chunks*
- *chilled green beans or asparagus spears*
- *cold cooked snow peas and sliced water chestnuts*

Chicken Breasts Diablo

CHICKEN 'N' SPICE—EASY 'N' NICE

This peppery chicken entree can be assembled quickly and cooks in minutes. Serve it with Parmesan-flavored artichoke hearts, fresh whole wheat rolls and a creamy chocolate dessert that you'll want to keep in mind for quick company meals.

Menu for 4

- **Chicken Breasts Diablo**
- **Artichoke Hearts Parmigiana**
- **Whole Wheat Rolls**
- **Speedy Chocolate Tarts**

SHOPPING LIST

- ☐ 4 chicken cutlets
- ☐ 1 4-ounce package instant chocolate pudding
- ☐ 1 small package chocolate chips
- ☐ 4 graham cracker tart shells
- ☐ 1 8-ounce container frozen whipped topping made with real cream
- ☐ Whole wheat rolls
- ☐ 2 9-ounce packages frozen artichoke hearts
- ☐ White crème de menthe

Have on Hand
- ☐ Salt
- ☐ Pepper

- ☐ Garlic
- ☐ Ground red pepper
- ☐ Dijon mustard
- ☐ Parmesan cheese
- ☐ Salad oil
- ☐ Olive oil
- ☐ 1 lemon or lemon juice
- ☐ Dry bread crumbs

SCHEDULE

1. Prepare Speedy Chocolate Tarts.
2. Prepare Artichoke Hearts Parmigiana.
3. Prepare Chicken Breasts Diablo.

Chicken Breasts Diablo

¼	cup Dijon mustard
½	teaspoon ground red pepper
½	teaspoon salt
4	chicken cutlets
½ to ¾	cup dry bread crumbs
3	tablespoons salad oil
1	teaspoon lemon juice

Combine mustard, red pepper and salt. Spread over both sides of chicken cutlets. Dip in bread crumbs.

In large skillet heat oil over high heat. Saute chicken about 3 minutes on each side or until brown. Drizzle on lemon juice.

Artichoke Hearts Parmigiana

2	tablespoons olive oil
2	large garlic cloves, minced
2	packages (9 oz. each) frozen artichoke hearts
¼	cup water
¼	teaspoon salt
⅛	teaspoon pepper
1	tablespoon grated Parmesan cheese

In large skillet heat olive oil. Add garlic; saute 1 minute. Add artichoke hearts, water, salt and pepper. Bring water to a boil. Cover; reduce heat and cook 8 minutes. Transfer to serving dish; sprinkle with grated Parmesan.

Speedy Chocolate Tarts

1	package (regular size) instant chocolate pudding
1	tablespoon white crème de menthe
4	graham cracker tart shells
1	cup frozen whipped topping made with real cream
4	tablespoons chocolate chips or shavings

Prepare instant chocolate pudding according to package directions, stirring in crème de menthe along with the milk. Pour into tart shells; refrigerate until serving time. Top with large dollops of whipped cream and sprinkle with chocolate chips or shavings.

ARTICHOKE HEARTS AND . . .

Cook a 9-ounce package of frozen artichoke hearts according to package directions. Drain well and toss with:

- *carrot chunks or slices, cooked just until tender*
- *buttered green beans*
- *tiny cooked shrimp*
- *crabmeat or surimi*
- *drained tuna chunks*
- *cubed ham*
- *chunks of chicken or turkey white meat*
- *pimiento strips and chopped ripe olives*

Sesame Pork Tenderloin

QUICK, DELICIOUS PORK MAIN DISH

Cook this whole pork tenderloin in your microwave oven in just fourteen minutes. Prepare the broccoli on top of the stove or follow the Tips for microwaving.

Menu for 6

- **Sesame Pork Tenderloin**
- **Shredded Sweet Potatoes**
- **Broccoli and Red Pepper Salad**

Sliced Pound Cake with Peaches

SHOPPING LIST

- ☐ 1½ pound whole pork tenderloin
- ☐ ½ pound sweet potatoes
- ☐ 1 bunch broccoli
- ☐ 1 red pepper
- ☐ 1 bunch green onions
- ☐ 1 small piece fresh ginger or ground ginger
- ☐ 4 peaches or 1 12-ounce package frozen sliced peaches
- ☐ 1 16-ounce can or bottle ginger ale
- ☐ 1 pound cake
- ☐ 1 small jar sesame seed

Have on Hand
- ☐ Salt
- ☐ Pepper
- ☐ Garlic
- ☐ Dry mustard
- ☐ Cinnamon
- ☐ Nutmeg
- ☐ Salad oil
- ☐ Cider vinegar
- ☐ Butter or margarine
- ☐ Soy sauce
- ☐ Dry sherry

SCHEDULE

1. Prepare Shredded Sweet Potatoes.
2. Prepare Sesame Pork Tenderloin.
3. Prepare Broccoli and Red Pepper Salad.

Sesame Pork Tenderloin

2   *tablespoons sesame seed*
1½ *pounds whole pork tenderloin*
⅔   *cup dry sherry*
½   *cup soy sauce*
½   *cup sliced green onions*
1   *tablespoon salad oil*
1   *garlic clove, minced*
1   *teaspoon minced fresh ginger or ¼ teaspoon ground*

In small microwave-proof dish spread sesame seed in a thin layer. Toast in microwave on High 5 minutes. Stir; set aside. Place pork in microwave-proof baking dish. Combine remaining ingredients; pour over pork. Sprinkle with sesame seed. Cover with plastic wrap; slit small hole on top. Cook on High 5 minutes. Turn dish and baste pork with sauce. Cover and cook on High 4 minutes.

Shredded Sweet Potatoes

¼   *cup butter or margarine*
½   *pound sweet potatoes, shredded*
¾   *cup ginger ale*
¼   *teaspoon cinnamon*
¼   *teaspoon nutmeg*
¼   *teaspoon salt*

In large skillet melt butter or margarine. Add shredded sweet potatoes; stir until coated. Add remaining ingredients. Reduce heat, cover and cook until tender, about 15 minutes.

Broccoli and Red Pepper Salad

4   *cups broccoli florets*
1   *red pepper, cut into 1-inch chunks*
2   *tablespoons chopped green onion*
¼   *cup salad oil*
2   *tablespoons cider vinegar*
½   *teaspoon salt*
¼   *teaspoon pepper*
¼   *teaspoon dry mustard*

Cook broccoli in salted water 5 to 7 minutes until just tender; plunge into cold water to cool. Toss florets with red pepper and green onion. In small jar with tight-fitting lid combine remaining ingredients; shake well and pour over salad. Toss again; refrigerate until serving time.

BROCCOLI TIPS

To cook in microwave: Arrange broccoli around outer rim of a microwave pie plate with stalks pointing toward outside edge. Add 2 tablespoons water; cover tightly. Microwave on High 2 to 3 minutes, until just tender. Plunge broccoli into cold water to cool.

For a tasty salad, toss cold cooked broccoli with vinaigrette and:
- *cubed leftover ham*
- *cold cooked whole-kernel corn*
- *chopped red pepper, blanched and chilled*
- *cold cooked rice or corkscrew pasta*

Spaghettini with Scallops

EASY, ELEGANT ITALIAN DINNER

Slender spaghettini cooks in minutes. Toss it with garlicky bay scallops and serve with a colorful vegetable and a refreshing salad.

Menu for 4

- **Spaghettini with Scallops**
- **Pan-Fried Zucchini and Yellow Squash**

Bibb Lettuce and Tomato Salad

Italian Bread

Red Grapes with Camembert Cheese

SHOPPING LIST

- ☐ 1 pound bay scallops
- ☐ ½ pound spaghettini
- ☐ 2 medium zucchini
- ☐ 1 medium yellow squash
- ☐ 1 head Bibb lettuce
- ☐ 2 tomatoes
- ☐ 1 bunch fresh parsley or dried parsley
- ☐ 1 large bunch red grapes
- ☐ 1 loaf Italian bread
- ☐ 1 small Camembert cheese

Have on Hand

- ☐ All-purpose flour
- ☐ Salt
- ☐ Pepper

- ☐ Garlic
- ☐ Salad oil
- ☐ Olive oil
- ☐ Bottled salad dressing
- ☐ Butter or margarine
- ☐ Dry white wine

SCHEDULE

1. Prepare salad.
2. Prepare Pan-Fried Zucchini and Yellow Squash.
3. Prepare Spaghettini with Scallops.
4. Arrange grapes with cheese.

Spaghettini with Scallops

½ *pound spaghettini*
½ *cup olive oil, divided*
1 *garlic clove, chopped*
1 *pound bay scallops*
½ *teaspoon salt*
¼ *teaspoon pepper*
½ *cup dry white wine*
2 *tablespoons finely chopped parsley*

Cook spaghettini according to package directions. Meanwhile, in skillet heat 2 tablespoons oil. Add garlic and saute 1 minute. Add scallops, salt and pepper. Saute, stirring frequently, 2 minutes or until scallops turn opaque. Add remaining oil, wine and parsley. Simmer, stirring frequently, 2 minutes more. Pour over well-drained pasta and toss.

Pan-Fried Zucchini and Yellow Squash

½ *cup all-purpose flour*
¼ *teaspoon salt*
⅛ *teaspoon pepper*
2 *medium zucchini, sliced*
1 *medium yellow squash, sliced*
3 *tablespoons butter or margarine*

1 *tablespoon salad oil*
1 *garlic clove, slightly crushed*

In paper or plastic bag combine flour, salt and pepper. Place zucchini and yellow squash slices in bag, a few at a time, and shake until lightly coated. In large skillet heat butter or margarine and oil. Add crushed garlic; saute 1 minute. Add zucchini and yellow squash; saute, turning occasionally, 10 to 12 minutes until tender but not mushy. Remove garlic.

QUICK SCALLOP ENTREES

Fresh scallops are tasty, nourishing, quick-cooking and versatile. Here are some cooking tips (for sea scallops, double the cooking time).

- *To pan-fry: Roll scallops in seasoned flour; fry quickly in hot oil until golden brown, 1 to 2 minutes.*
- *To broil: Place scallops in greased baking dish; dot with butter and season to taste. Sprinkle with paprika and broil 3 to 4 minutes until opaque.*
- *To poach: In saucepan place 1 whole onion and a sprig of parsley. Add 3 cups water and ½ cup dry white wine; bring to a boil. Add scallops and simmer 1 to 2 minutes.*

Stir-Fried Chicken and Vegetables

CHICKEN WITH CRUNCHY SPRING VEGETABLES

Stir-frying is fast, saves energy, and offers delicious results. We know you'll love this chicken-vegetable combination. Serve with fluffy rice and a smooth fruit dessert you can prepare with whatever fruit your family prefers. If you use slightly overripe bananas for this whipped delight, it will taste even better.

Menu for 4

- **Stir-Fried Chicken and Vegetables**

  Rice
- **Fresh Fruit Whip**

SHOPPING LIST

- ☐ 4   chicken cutlets
- ☐ ¼   pound snow peas
- ☐ 1   large red pepper
- ☐ 8   asparagus spears
- ☐ 1   small piece fresh ginger
- ☐ 1   or 2 very ripe bananas
- ☐ 1   pint strawberries or 2 fresh peaches or nectarines
- ☐ 1   small can water chestnuts
- ☐ 1   8-ounce container plain yogurt

Have on Hand
- ☐ Long-grain rice
- ☐ Sugar

- ☐ Cornstarch
- ☐ Garlic
- ☐ Salad oil
- ☐ Wine vinegar
- ☐ Red pepper flakes
- ☐ Soy sauce
- ☐ Dry sherry

SCHEDULE

1. Cook rice.
2. Prepare Stir-Fried Chicken and Vegetables.
3. Prepare Fresh Fruit Whip.

Stir-Fried Chicken and Vegetables

3   tablespoons soy sauce,
       divided
2   tablespoons plus 2 tea-
       spoons dry sherry,
       divided
4   chicken cutlets, cut into
       1-inch cubes
3   tablespoons salad oil,
       divided
¼   pound snow peas
1   red pepper, cut into 1-inch
       squares
8   asparagus spears
½   cup sliced water
       chestnuts
2   large garlic cloves, finely
       chopped
1   to 1 ½ teaspoons finely
       chopped ginger
2   tablespoons water
1   tablespoon sugar
2   teaspoons wine
       vinegar
2   teaspoons cornstarch
¼   to ½ teaspoon red pepper
       flakes

In small bowl combine 1 tablespoon soy sauce and 2 teaspoons dry sherry. Toss with chicken. In skillet heat 1 tablespoon salad oil. Add vegetables and water chestnuts; stir to coat with oil. Cover; cook 1 minute. Uncover and cook, stirring, 1 minute. Remove from skillet. To same skillet add remaining oil. Add chicken; stir-fry quickly, about 2 minutes. Add garlic and ginger; cook 1 minute. In small bowl combine remaining soy sauce and dry sherry with next 5 ingredients. Return vegetables to skillet; increase heat to high. Add sauce. Cook, stirring constantly, until sauce thickens.

Fresh Fruit Whip

1   cup plain yogurt
1   cup ice cubes
1   or 2 very ripe
       bananas
1   cup strawberries or sliced
       peaches or nectarines

In blender combine all ingredients. Cover and blend until smooth. Serve immediately.

CHICKEN STIR-FRY VARIATIONS

Next time, in place of snow peas, red peppers and asparagus, stir-fry the following vegetables with chicken chunks:
- *broccoli florets*
- *onion wedges*
- *fresh mushrooms*
- *dried Chinese mushrooms (soaked in warm water about 20 minutes, until soft)*
- *cauliflower florets*
- *water chestnuts*
- *green pepper chunks*

Broiled Ginger Shrimp

CHINESE SAMPLER THAT'S SURE TO PLEASE

Here is a speedy Cantonese feast. Try to find bok choy for the soy-flavored vegetables, although broccoli will do nicely if the Asian product is not available. Ginger-flavored shrimp is this menu's main dish, but keep it in mind as skewered finger food for your next party.

Menu for 4

Egg Rolls
- Broiled Ginger
  Shrimp
  Rice
- Stir-Fried
  Vegetables

Green Tea Ice
Cream or Lime
Sherbet and
Fortune
Cookies

SHOPPING LIST

- 1 pound shrimp
- 1 head bok choy or broccoli
- 2 medium carrots
- 2 small red peppers
- 1 small piece fresh ginger
- 1 small package fortune cookies
- 1 pint green tea ice cream or
     lime sherbet

Have on Hand
- Long-grain rice
- Garlic
- Distilled white vinegar

- Peanut or salad oil
- Soy sauce
- Nonstick vegetable spray
- Dry vermouth

SCHEDULE

1. Prepare egg rolls.
2. Cook rice.
3. Prepare Stir-Fried Vegetables.
4. Prepare Broiled Ginger Shrimp.

Broiled Ginger Shrimp

½   cup dry vermouth
¼   cup soy sauce
1½ teaspoons sugar
¾   teaspoon minced fresh
     ginger
1   pound shrimp, shelled
     and deveined
     Nonstick vegetable spray

In small saucepan combine vermouth, soy sauce, sugar and ginger. Bring to a boil. Remove from heat.

Split shrimp down back without cutting through; flatten. Marinate 10 minutes. Preheat broiler. Spray broiler pan with nonstick vegetable spray. Remove shrimp from marinade and place on broiler pan. Broil shrimp 3 inches from heat 2 to 3 minutes on each side.

Stir-Fried Vegetables

1   head bok choy or broccoli
     (4 cups chopped)
2   tablespoons peanut or
     salad oil
1   garlic clove, crushed
1½ medium carrots, thinly
     sliced
2   small red peppers, cut
     into 1-inch pieces
2   tablespoons soy sauce
     Pinch sugar

Cut bok choy diagonally into 1-inch pieces, keeping stalks separate from leafy green pieces. (For broccoli, trim off and discard woody ends. Peel stems and cut diagonally into ¼-inch slices. Separate florets into bite-size pieces.)

In medium skillet or wok heat oil over medium-high heat. Add garlic and cook until browned; remove. Add carrots and peppers; stir-fry 2 minutes, stirring frequently. Add stalks of bok choy or broccoli and stir-fry 1 minute. Reduce heat; cover and cook 1 to 2 minutes more. Add remaining ingredients and stir to combine.

COOKING WITH CHINESE INGREDIENTS

Bean sprouts, tofu, water chestnuts, bok choy and many other tasty and unusual Chinese products are now widely available. Try some of these foods, too.

- *Bamboo shoots: Add to stir-fried meat or vegetables for lightness and texture.*
- *Five-spice powder: Add sparingly to stir-fried shrimp or chicken.*
- *Litchi nuts: Serve for dessert with fortune cookies.*
- *Dried Chinese mushrooms: Soak in warm water 20 minutes; add to meat or vegetables with soaking liquid.*

Barbecued Chicken

SPEEDY MICROWAVE MAIN DISH

A zesty barbecue sauce adds delectable flavor to this chicken entree. Serve it with a beautiful arrangement of carrots, beans and squash. We think you'll find that even the most determined vegetable-hater will succumb to this microwave delight.

Menu for 4

- **Quick and Zesty Barbecued Chicken Rice**

- **Vegetable Platter with Dill Butter Cherry Pie**

SHOPPING LIST

- ☐ 1 3-pound chicken, cut up
- ☐ 2 large carrots
- ☐ ½ pound green beans
- ☐ 1 yellow squash
- ☐ 1 small zucchini
- ☐ 1 small onion
- ☐ ¼ pound mushrooms
- ☐ 1 bunch parsley or dried parsley
- ☐ 1 bunch fresh dill or dillweed
- ☐ 1 cherry pie

Have on Hand
- ☐ Long-grain rice
- ☐ Brown sugar
- ☐ Salt
- ☐ Pepper

- ☐ Garlic
- ☐ 1 lemon or lemon juice
- ☐ Salad oil
- ☐ Cider vinegar
- ☐ Soy sauce
- ☐ Red pepper sauce
- ☐ Ketchup
- ☐ Butter or margarine

SCHEDULE

1. Cook rice.
2. Prepare Quick and Zesty Barbecued Chicken.
3. Prepare Vegetable Platter with Dill Butter.

Quick and Zesty Barbecued Chicken

2   tablespoons salad oil
1   garlic clove, minced
1   small onion, finely
     chopped
½   cup ketchup
2   tablespoons brown
     sugar
2   tablespoons soy sauce
1   tablespoon lemon juice
1   tablespoon cider
     vinegar
½   teaspoon red pepper
     sauce
1   chicken (3 lbs.), cut up
¼   teaspoon salt
⅛   teaspoon pepper

In 4-cup glass measure combine oil, garlic and onion. Microwave on High 2 to 3 minutes, until vegetables are tender. Stir in remaining ingredients. Microwave uncovered on High 5 minutes to thicken slightly, stirring once. Set aside.

In 2-quart rectangular microwave dish place chicken skin side down, with thicker portions to the outside. Cover with wax paper. Microwave on High 18 minutes, turning and placing less cooked areas to the outside halfway through.

Remove chicken; sprinkle with salt and pepper and baste with sauce. Grill chicken or broil 4 to 5 minutes per side or until crisp, basting with sauce. Serve remaining barbecue sauce with chicken.

Vegetable Platter with Dill Butter

2   large carrots, cut into
     ¼-inch slices
½   pound green beans,
     trimmed and halved
1   yellow squash, cut into
     ¼-inch slices
1   small zucchini, cut into
     ¼-inch slices
¼   pound mushrooms, sliced
2   tablespoons butter
2   tablespoons chopped
     parsley
1   tablespoon chopped fresh
     dill or 1 teaspoon
     dillweed
1   tablespoon lemon juice

Arrange carrots in a circle around outer rim of a 10- to 12-inch round microwave platter, overlapping slightly. Repeat in concentric circles with green beans, squash and zucchini. Spoon mushrooms in center. Sprinkle with 2 tablespoons water. Cover tightly. Microwave on High 5 to 7 minutes, until vegetables are tender, rotating dish once. Let stand covered 2 minutes.

In 1-cup measure combine butter, parsley, dill and lemon juice. Microwave on High 1 minute or until melted. Stir and pour over vegetables.

MICROWAVE TIP

• *To warm up refrigerated pies, microwave 30 to 45 seconds.*

Index

For information on how to subscribe to
Ladies' Home Journal, please write to:

Ladies' Home Journal
Box 10895
Des Moines, IA 50336-0895